Nazi Evil

Hitler and Mengele

2 Books in 1

Anna Revell

Table of Contents

After World War II Mengele Goes to South America

America

Mengele's Legacy

HITLER

A Biography of Evil
The Life and Times of the Most Evil
Man in History, Adolf Hitler

Anna Revell

The Rejected Artist

In 1908 a young man left the Academy of Fine Arts in Vienna. The 19 year old youth was bitterly disappointed. He had sought a place in that august institution, and had been rejected – for the second time.

The young man's name was Adolf Hitler. He was the son of a customs official, Alois Hitler, a harsh, overbearing figure who beat him and with whom Adolf constantly fought. Alois died in 1903.

Klara, Adolf's mother, was by contrast a kind and affectionate woman. When she died of breast cancer in 1908 he was inconsolable, having lost probably the only meaningful relationship in his life.

Adolf left school in 1905 with dreams of being a painter. But the Academy had dismissed his application, citing his 'unfitness for painting.'

Despondent and penniless, Adolf eked meagre living painting watercolors in Vienna, often relying on soup kitchens vagrant shelters.

His paintings have been described as competent, but certainly not outstanding. Hitler maintained his interest in art throughout his life. He painted in quiet moments during World War I

In later years he would see art purely as an expression of the political will.

Life in Vienna was hard. Without money and prospects, the young Hitler lived on charity and luck. His dreams were dashed and he had nothing to hope for.

Vienna at this time was the capital of the Austro-Hungarian Empire. Austria and Hungary, united under Franz Joseph I of the ancient House of Habsburg, together ruled a hotchpotch of ethnicities: Germans, Magyars, Romanians, Poles, Slavs, Czechs, Slovaks, Slovenians, Italians and Romanians.

Hungary was dominated by the Magyars, and in Austria the Germans ruled.

To the north of Austria was the great German Empire or Reich. In 1871 the powerful Kingdom of Prussia, ruled by the

Hohenzollern dynasty, had united all of Germany.

All Germany that is, except for Austria which remained under Habsburg rule. The German nationalist movement, which baulked at having been excluded from the German Reich, was growing in Vienna at the time Hitler was on its streets.

The most prominent advocate of union with Germany was George Ritter Schonerer.

A gifted and fiery orator, Schonerer (1842 - 1921) was elected to Austria's parliament, the Imperial Council, and denounced the anti-German, Catholic Habsburg regime.

Schonerer went on to form his own party, the Pan-German party. His vision for a greater Germany did not include the Jews. He maintained that a Jew could not be a good German.

Schonerer was certainly not alone in his contempt for the Jews. Anti-Semitism figured in the writings of many European intellectuals during the nineteenth century.

A French Jew, Alfred Dreyfus, was accused of leaking military secrets in the 1890s. The Czars of Russia periodically and systematically persecuted Russian Jews.

A forged document, entitled The Protocols of the Elders of Zion was published in 1903. It purports to set forth a plan for the subversion of Christian Europe to Jewish control. It was read widely and continues to circulate today.

In this environment Schonerer's ideas and personality gripped many young minds in Austria. Hitler's was one of them.

Hitler, disillusioned and aimless, had at last an idea that could inspire him. He wrote in his memoir, Mein Kampf, 'I ceased to be a weak-kneed cosmopolitan and became an anti-Semite ... at this time of bitter struggle; the streets of Vienna had provided valuable instruction.'

In 1914 the black clouds of war were hanging over Europe. A number of diplomatic crises had brought the Great Powers – Austria-

Hungary, France, Germany, Great Britain and France - to the brink of war.

On these occasions these countries had pulled back from the edge just in time. Yet there was the feeling that conflict was inevitable. Nations sharpened their swords and called their youth to the colors.

Adolf Hitler was ordered to attend an army conscription station to be examined. He was declared physically unfit for service. Perhaps reeling from the blow, Hitler left the Austro-Hungarian Empire for his father's estate in Munich, Bavaria.

The Soldier

On June 28 1914 an Austro-Hungarian archduke who happened to be heir to the imperial throne, Franz Ferdinand, was shot and killed, along with his wife, by Serbian nationalists in the town of Sarajevo in Bosnia-Herzegovina.

A short period of frantic diplomatic exchanges began, followed by mobilization of troops by the Great Powers. Austria-Hungary declared war on Serbia on July 28. Declarations of war cascaded one after another, and by August 4 all the Great Powers were at war.

Austria-Hungary and the German Empire were allied against France, Great Britain and

Russia. The moribund Turkish Empire and Bulgaria later joined the former. The United States, Italy, Romania and Greece would join the latter.

The youth of Europe joined the colors with a joyous abandonment that seems incomprehensible to us today. The young Hitler, living in Munich, was likewise fired with zeal for Germany's cause, and sought to enlist in the Bavarian Army.

Hitler was still an Austrian citizen but he was allowed to enlist. Bavarian officials were later to question how a non-German citizen could join the imperial German forces.

The 25 year old Hitler was assigned to the 16th Bavarian Reserve Regiment. He saw action in Belgium at the First Battle of Ypres in October 1914.

During this battle almost a half of the newly recruited German troops perished. Hitler's own regiment lost five sixth's of its men, including the commander.

Afterwards Private Hitler was made a corporal and regimental message runner on the Western Front. In this capacity he often found time to paint and read politics.

As a messenger Hitler was privy to military planning, discussions, orders and intelligence. This was considered by many to be a cushy job, since it took its incumbent away from the combat zone.

Hitler's soldier friend's regarded him as an individual who liked to keep to himself. He never complained and never talked about women. He never drank and hardly wrote letters home. He had a most unmilitary bearing, and, although brave, seemed to have a knack for avoiding injury.

In later years Hitler would make a great deal of his war experiences, lauding himself to his generals and party colleagues, especially when they were trying to tell him that his military strategies would not work.

Hitler was not an outstanding soldier, despite being awarded five medals, including the Iron Cross First Class in 1918. His officers would not recommend him for promotion to sergeant, believing him to lack the leadership qualities required.

His Iron Cross, which Hitler would wear with pride all his life, was awarded for service as a messenger.

Historians have questioned whether this medal, hardly ever awarded to someone of Hitler's rank, was truly merited. After all, taking messages from HQ to the front lines was his job, and the citation does not mention any specific incident that might have merited it.

It has been suggested that the awarding of the Iron Cross was a mistake. Whatever the circumstances, it seemed to seal Hitler's later belief that he was a war hero, and the man best suited to lead Germany into war.

Ironically, the officer who recommended Hitler for decoration was a Jew named Hugo Gutmann. In 1937 Gutmann was imprisoned by the Gestapo, but some SS officers who knew his connection to Hitler procured his release.

Hitler himself never mentioned Gutman when referring to his war service.

Two other incidents in Hitler's military career bear repeating. They throw light on Hitler's attitude to the war.

On Christmas Day 1914 German and Allied troops ceased firing at each other. Instead they greeted each other, exchange gifts, sang carols, and even played football.

This extraordinary gesture, affirming life over death, even if it was for just one day, signaled hope, as it still does today, that mutual respect might overcome the futility of conflict.

Hitler did not participate in the celebrations. For him, truce was weakness. Fraternization was treachery.

The other incident occurred on November 10 1918. Hitler had been temporarily blinded in a gas attack near Ypres, and was recuperating in a Berlin hospital.

In Berlin he heard of the despondency and war-weariness of the German people, including the soldiers. He despised this kind of behavior, labelling it defeatism and attributing it to the influence of the Jews and Marxists.

An elderly clergyman came to the hospital and announced that Germany had surrendered. The Kaiser had abdicated and the government had signed an armistice on the terms of the Allies. The war was over.

Hitler wrote about the incident in Mein Kampf: 'There followed terrible days and even worse nights – I knew that all was lost … in these nights hatred grew in me, hatred for those responsible for this deed.'

Revenge

Germany had been utterly humiliated. No Allied army had actually invaded Germany, but the Army was demoralized and lacking in supplies and reinforcements. The people and the government had no stomach for continuing the conflict.

Over four years the German military lost over 2 million, that is, over 4% of the population of the Empire. Another 2 million or more had been wounded.

Britain, France, the United States and their allies had suffered comparable losses, but they had reinforcements. They had the economic resources to keep fighting.

Germany was the subject of a naval blockade, depriving it of trade.

At the end of October 1918 a Marxist revolution broke out throughout Germany, similar to the revolution that had broken out, and succeeded, in Russia a year before.

The German High Command, which in effect ruled Germany, handed over its power to the elected federal parliament or Reichstag. The Chancellor of Germany, Prince Maximillian, announced the Kaiser's abdication and handed power over to the moderate socialist, Friedrich Ebert.

The military and the upper classes agreed to support the new liberal regime as the only way to defeat the Marxists at home and negotiate with the Allies.

The Allies agreed to an armistice on the condition that they dictate the terms. The Germans were to have no negotiating power.

The Allied terms were laid down in the Treaty of Versailles, which Germany signed on June 28 1919.

The Treaty was deliberately designed to humiliate Germany, primarily at the instigation of the French.

It was signed in the opulent Hall of Mirrors in the Palace of Versailles near Paris. It was in this same place that the French had accepted Prussia's terms after the Franco-Prussian War in 1871.

Germany lost large amounts of its territory, mostly in the east and to the newly created state of Poland. In the west, Alsace-Lorraine, taken from France in the Franco-Prussian War, was restored to France.

Germany also lost the mineral-rich Saar region and its overseas colonies.

The most humiliating clause of the Treaty was the so-called 'guilt' clause, by which Germany was forced to accept responsibility for the war and pay reparations to the Allies.

The French wanted the treaty to be even more humiliating, but it was only the intervention of the British and the United States that stayed their hand.

The German High Command and government believed that they had no choice but to accept Versailles.

Much of the populace, however, and many politicians, especially of the Right, looked for explanations outside the battlefield.

The myth arose that the German Army had been undefeated: that it was betrayal by the government and by the High Command that forced the peace and imposed Versailles.

This was patently incorrect, but many looked for scapegoats: an unpatriotic populace, the military leadership, the Socialists, the

Bolsheviks, the Kaiser himself – and, of course, the age old scapegoat, the Jew.

The myth was helped in no small part by the first President of the Weimar Republic (named after the city where it's Constitution was drafted), Ebert, who greeted returning soldiers with the words 'no enemy has vanquished you.'

The reality of the situation was very different. The German Army had in fact suffered debilitating defeats in the last months of the war. The Empire did not possess the resources to continue the war. Its ally, Austria-Hungary had dissolved almost overnight in early November 1918.

Germany faced defeat abroad and revolution at home (a revolution begun by soldiers). Most historians agree that the German government had no practical choice but to accept an armistice.

However, masses experiencing pain are generally uninterested in reasoned explanations. For many, Germany must have lost the war because they were betrayed at home.

Adolf Hitler remained in the army after the war. After all, he had no formal qualifications and no prospects. He was politically charged and seeking an outlet for his growing hatred for those he perceived as the enemies of Germany.

Hitler was assigned to army intelligence in Munich. His assignment was to infiltrate and report on one of the many socialistic political organizations that had sprung up across Germany and were deemed subversive by the Army.

He infiltrated the German Workers' Party (DAP) in July 1919. The party had been founded earlier in the year on nationalistic and anti-Semitic principles.

The DAP arose out of the same political tradition that had produced Schonerer. It was nationalist, socialist, and anti-Semitic, and opposed to Germany's acquiescence in the Treaty of Versailles.

Anton Drexler, a Munich locksmith, founder of the Fatherland Front, joined minds with a right-wing journalist Karl Harrer to form the DAP.

In the beginning the party had few more than the 40 members that Drexler brought with him. It had no clear focus and no solid direction, largely confining itself to discussions in Bavarian beer halls (large pubs that specialize in beer).

It is to be wondered then why the German Army was interested in infiltrating the DAP. Nevertheless Hitler attended its meetings, with the intention of learning more about its agenda.

He seems to have been unimpressed by its lack of vigour and prowess. He was however impressed by its political ideals, which coincided strikingly with his own.

On September 12, Hitler found himself involved in a heated discussion about Bavaria's place in a revived Germany. One of the members suggested that Bavaria should split with the rest of Germany and unite with its neighbor Austria.

Hitler, enraged, took over the meeting and argued for 15 minutes, uninterrupted, that Germany must reclaim its place in Europe as a united country.

The assembly was mesmerized. After the meeting Drexler approached Hitler and invited him to study his ideas and to return.

Hitler regarded the DPAP as an 'absurd little organization.' However he acknowledged that by involving himself with the group he might find the political opportunity, and discipline, that he felt he needed. Here at last was a group that shared his ideas. Moreover, it was a young group that he could influence, perhaps even mould.

After only two days' deliberation he decided to accept a place on the DPAP Committee. He called it 'the most decisive resolve of my life.'

With the backing of Drexler, Hitler, with his talent for oratory, became the chief voice of this rag tag of a party. By 1920 it could hold meetings in front of as many as 2000 people.

In the same year he was discharged from the army and began to devote himself full-time to the cause.

In these formative years Hitler expounded his political doctrines clearly and without dissimulation.

He proclaimed that the Jews must not only be excluded from political and social life, but removed from society altogether.

Hitler was intensely anti-Marxist. The DPAP was a workers' party, and it would be renamed at Hitler's insistence the National Socialist German Workers' Party (NAZI) in 1920. However the kind of socialism it advocated was state-controlled based on the superiority of the German people, and not on re-distribution of wealth.

Hitler demanded that the principle of Fuhrerprinzip be followed. This was defined as unquestioning obedience to the leader of the party (who at this stage was still Drexler).

In the nineteenth century Shonerer also used the designation Fuhrer for himself.

At this time the swastika was adopted as the party emblem. The swastika is an ancient Indian symbol of spiritual power adopted by many cultures, including Christian. In fact many of the countries who would fight Nazism in World War II used it as a symbol of good fortune.

The Nazi Party adopted the swastika as an emblem of the Aryan people. They believe that the German people were descended from the white Aryans who migrated from India and gave rise to the European peoples.

Nazis believed that the race only remained pure in the Teutonic or Germanic peoples, which included the English and Scandinavian peoples.

Hitler also adopted the now infamous Nazi salute. At the time however it was called the Roman salute, after Benito Mussolini's

Italian fascists. Ironically, there is no evidence that the Ancient Romans ever practiced the salute in the way the fascists of the twentieth century did.

The greeting 'heil' ('hail') was already popular in the German nationalist movement, of which Drexler's National Socialists was only one component amongst many.

It was only when Hitler assumed the leadership of Germany in 1933 that heil was joined to Hitler's own name.

Hitler was drawing new members into the Nazi Party. Even at this time, membership was restricted to individuals of proven Aryan descent.

But although his oratory drove the party and gained it a public audience there were still only 190 actual members in 1920 and Hitler was not Fuhrer of the Party.

This changed in June 1921. While Hitler was in Berlin on party business the executive committee, Drexler included, voted to merge with its rival, the German Socialist Party.

Many of the members of the nascent Nazi Party feared and resented Hitler's influence and saw a merger as a means of disempowering him.

Hitler was furious, and resigned. The committee had not foreseen this, and realized that the party was doomed without him.

Hitler told the committee that he would only return if he replaced Drexler as Chairman of the Executive Committee.

The Party agreed. Drexler was to remain as honorary President. But Hitler had his eyes on that position too. He meant to be the undisputed leader of the Party – and beyond.

Mein Kampf

In October of 1922 in Italy about 30 000 armed members of the National Fascist Party, led by an obscure journalist, Benito Mussolini, marched on Rome and demanded power. King Victor Emmanuel III, fearing civil war, gave him the government.

Hitler and other national socialists in Germany looked upon these events with elation and envy. Like German nationalism, Italian fascism called for the union of all nationals, wherever they were, under one government.

Like German National Socialism, it called for a totalitarian regime under a single ruler.

It is also called for laws to safeguard racial purity and exclude Jews from active participation in society.

Hitler was inspired to emulate Mussolini's daring. The seizure of the entire German state was too ambitious, too premature. He did believe however that he could take control of the federal state of Bavaria.

The German Republic was in a state of crisis, as it had been since its inception. There had been six Chancellors in four years. Politics was dominated by the Social Democratic Party, blamed by the Right for the so-called 'stab in the back' of Germany in 1918.

The war reparations demanded by Treaty of Versailles was handicapping the economy and in 1923 the government started defaulting.

Inflation had reached such a level that one US dollar was worth over four trillion papier mark. There were workers strikes and the number of unemployed swelled.

The government was under attack from both the nationalist Right and Marxist Left. Outbreaks of violence from either side were dealt with in kind.

At the beginning of November Hitler believed the time was right for a coup, or putsch, in Munich. From Munich he would take Berlin and overthrow the government.

He elicited the support of Erich Ludendorff, a prominent general in World War I, who led an offensive that came close to capturing Paris just months before the 1918 Armistice.

Bands of armed national socialist thugs joined the conspiracy, as well as many unemployed men.

On the evening of November 8 Adolf Hitler marched on a popular Beer Hall at the head of the SA, the newly created military arm of the Nazi Party.

With the words 'the national revolution has broken out' he declared the Bavarian government deposed. He then confronted the State Commissioner of Bavaria, Gustav von Kahr, who had been addressing a meeting.

Hitler demanded that Kahr join him. Kahr's political convictions were very similar to Hitler's. However he refused. He and his officers were detained but were later released. They were to rally opposition to Hitler.

The crowd in the beer hall loudly cheered Hitler and Ludendorff.

Despite the enthusiasm of the crowd (who had been told they could not leave until Hitler's SA allowed them to do so) the Bavarian state representatives present could not agree on whom to support.

Hitler knew he had to act fast, but this indecision allowed the state to organize its counterattack. By 3 am the Army and the Police were engaging the armed fascist bands.

When the morning of November 9 dawned, Hitler had lost control of the situation. His supporters did not know what to do, whereas the state forces were well-organized and well led.

In desperation Hitler asked Crown Prince Ruprecht of Bavaria, son of the deposed King of Bavaria, to intervene on his behalf, promising to restore the Crown of Bavaria. But Ruprecht dismissed Hitler as insane.

It was Ludendorff who took control, and ordered a march on the Bavarian Defense Ministry.

Two thousand men met 130 state soldiers. There was a battle. Four state policemen fell, and 16 Nazis. Hitler himself was wounded.

The putsch had failed. On November 12 Hitler was arrested, along with a number of his co-conspirators. Most of the Nazis managed to escape, many to Austria.

Hitler was tried in 1924. Despite the failure of the putsch Hitler still had his supporters in the government, and Nazi sympathizers were appointed as judges.

These judges allowed Hitler to speak at length without interruption, interrupt witnesses and even cross-examine them.

Far from deny the charge of treason, Hitler justified his actions and took sole responsibility for them.

Newspapers related Hitler's courtroom speeches, and people all over Germany read them. Hitler had long realized that he could use any situation, however seemingly disadvantageous, to gain an audience.

Hitler boldly told the court that history would acquit him. There were already judges who wanted to acquit right then and there. However, a guilty verdict was returned on April 1 1924.

The sentence was five years, and could have been life. He was imprisoned at an old fortress in Landsberg, if imprisonment is the right word.

He had a spacious, well-furnished cell. He received gifts from supporters and was allowed to receive visitors. He even had his own private secretary, fellow conspirator and detainee, Rudolf Hess.

Ludendorff was acquitted on account of the esteem in which he was held.

While in prison Hitler wrote or rather dictated to Hess, a book known as Mein Kampf (My Struggle).

In this book Hitler talks about his upbringing, youth, and membership in the Nazi Party.

However it is mostly an exposition of his ideas about race, the future of Germany, the cause of Germany's fall, and what a world dominated by Germany should look like.

In this book we do not see a man trying to make sense of the world in a reasoned manner. Rather we read the ramblings of someone who sees the world through a series of prejudices regarding race and history.

In Mein Kampf Hitler proclaims the superiority of the Aryan race, of which the Germans are the most perfect expression.

He arrogantly asserts that Germany 'should demand the subordination of the inferior' and that true human culture is 'almost exclusively the creative product of the Aryan.'

If the German race is the highest then, he says, the Jewish race must be 'the mightiest counterpart'. He presents the world as a battleground between Aryanism and Judaism, the latter being responsible for everything that is corrupt, including Marxism and liberal democracy.

He does not offer any proof for any of this, as if he believes he does not need to. He holds it to be simply a fact.

It is well to remember that Hitler was proclaiming this quite openly. He had a ready audience, not only in the National Socialist Movement, but in a sizeable portion of the German population.

We should also be aware that anti-Semitism was the mindset of many outside of Germany as well. Hitler's beliefs were reflected by many across Europe and the world, including in the United Kingdom and USA.

Indeed, antisemitism is on the rise again in the present day.

Mein Kampf presents what Hitler sees as the National Socialist vision for Europe.

First, the Treaty of Versailles was to be repudiated. All of Germany's territories and its military were to be restored. Austria was to be united with Germany. The territories given to Poland were to be restored.

Secondly, there would be a war of revenge against France. Then an invasion of Russia and the enslavement of the inferior Slavs in order to obtain lebensraum (living space) for the Aryans.

In this world there is no room for the Jews. There is however no hint in the book of the horrible fate that awaited them.

Hitler's agenda was proclaimed unequivocally and clearly. Yet when he came to power few people looked back to Mein Kampf as his stated program for action.

Beginning Again

When Hitler was released, just before Christmas 1924, barely nine months after he was sentenced for five years, he had learnt from his mistakes.

From now on he would not try to topple the government by violence. Instead he would become the government. He would participate in the democratic process he hated so much by fielding National Socialist German Workers' Party candidates for election to the Reichstag (national parliament).

There were obstacles. The Nazi Party had been abolished in Bavaria. Hitler went to the

Bavarian Prime Minister and convinced him to lift the ban.

Bizarrely, Hitler's promises of good behavior were accepted.

But soon Hitler was lambasting the Jews, Socialists and democrats again. This time the government banned him from public speaking for two years.

Hitler used his time of silence to reorganize the Nazi Party.

He created a government in waiting, a political structure that could be imposed overnight. It consisted of 34 districts; each governed by a gaulitier, with Hitler, the Fuhrer, of course on top.

He also organized Hitler Youth to teach boys 'Aryan' values.

Hitler also restructured the paramilitary wing of the Nazi Party.

The SA, or Sturmabteilung, had unsuccessfully supported Hitler in the Beer Hall Putsch. It arose from a group of loosely organized thugs used to protect officers of the Nazi Part at political meetings.

Within the SA Hitler created an elite force which acted as his personal body guard. They wore a black uniform and were called the Schutzstaffel, or SS.

The main obstacle to the rise of the Nazi Party in Germany was the success of the government.

Things were turning around. The Centre (Catholic) Party had taken political dominance from the Social Democrats and succeeded in forming a coalition government. Unemployment was falling. The economy was booming.

Investment poured in from the United States. The factories were opening again. War reparations were reduced and the German currency was stabilizing.

In 1925 the election of the war leader General Paul von Hindenburg as President gave Germany the stability it so desperately needed. Hindenburg united the conservatives and the centrists in government.

The radicals, both of the left and the right, were excluded. There was no room for the Nazis.

Even the hated Treaty of Versailles was being covertly repudiated. Armed paramilitary forces were making up for the forces Germany was not supposed to have.

Importantly, the German High Command and Army, long used to a position of influence in German society, had been elevated, through the President, to the highest station. It supported the government.

It appeared that the Republic was finally secure.

In these days of complacency the name of Adolf Hitler produced but a smirk. The Beer Hall Putsch; the odd military uniforms; those funny salutes – these were surely the expressions of powerless cranks.

In 1926 the Nazi Party numbered only 17000 members, and Hitler was still forbidden to speak.

Hitler could not speak, but others could. The most powerful of the Nazi propagandists was Joseph Goebbels. Highly educated and gifted, Goebbels met Hitler at this time.

Goebbels was instantly captivated by Hitler and professed undying devotion. His devotion lasted until the very hour Hitler died.

In 1926 Hitler gave Goebbels the task of re-organizing the Party in Berlin. This was a huge task, especially in view of the political stability in the capital.

In Berlin he made sure the Nazi Party was noticed, by propaganda, the Press, and by violence.

When Hitler's time of silence was over he joined Goebbels in Berlin and spoke to a crowd of 5000 supporters.

The first results for the Nazis in the 1927 General Election were poor. But in 1929 a world event was to occur that would change their fortunes.

The Road to Power

On October 29 1929 Wall Street crashed. Banks failed, companies went bankrupt, and the savings of millions of people across the world vanished overnight.

There was massive unemployment. The populace in such cities as New York, London and Paris lined up for bread and soup.

The German economy was especially vulnerable, since it had been growing on foreign capital, most of it from the United States.

With capital shrinking, the economy of Germany collapsed. Workers were laid off. Banks closed. Inflation returned.

Hitler, ever the opportunist, welcomed this terrible misery. He knew people would be seeking solutions. It would be easy to convince voters that the government had failed them.

The Jews and socialists were, as always in Hitler's mind, the cause of the trouble. Many Germans began to listen to the Nazis.

The previously strong and united government was falling apart. The factions in the Reichstag could not agree on how to deal with the crisis, and so, little happened.

Heinrich Bruning was appointed Chancellor in March 1930 with a plan for financial reform. Bruning was from the Centre Party, but the government could no longer govern from the Centre. The Reichstag resisted his plans.

President Hindenburg stepped in. Article 48 of the German Constitution allowed the president emergency powers. Bruning asked Hindenburg to promulgate his reforms without the consent of the Reichstag.

The Reichstag annulled the decree, as it had the right to do, by a small majority. Hindenburg then dissolved the Reichstag and ordered new elections.

Hitler immediately set to work. He travelled the country, giving speeches, holding rallies and meeting citizens.

He employed much the same tactics as politicians do today. He used catchphrases, promised jobs, a higher standard of living, but was short on detail.

Theatre was important to Hitler – as again, it is with politicians today. His rallies were marked by processions of brown-shirted party members bearing banners and shouting 'heil'!

Hitler used his skills in oratory to manipulate his audiences, driving them into a patriotic frenzy and causing them, as he hoped, to abandon reason and reflection.

Again we may say, not so far removed from the tactics of many politicians today.

There was no denying the appeal of the Nazi Party. Hitler promised jobs for workers, profits for companies, power to the Army, social equality.

He promised to tear up the Treaty of Versailles and to restore the glory of Germany. He would put Germany first, and make it great again.

And as ever, he was unashamedly open about his policy toward Jews and the Socialists – they were to be suppressed.

On September 14 1930 the Nazis won eighteen per cent of the national vote. This entitled them to 107 seats in the Reichstag. It was the second largest party in that assembly.

In the Reichstag the Nazi deputies answered their names with 'heil Hitler!' SA members in civilian dress celebrated their victory by smashing the windows of Jewish homes and shops.

President Hindenburg continued to exercise emergency powers. Bruning still needed those powers to pass his financial reforms. The Social Democrats, promising not to repudiate their use, was the only major party supporting the government.

Hindenburg and Hitler disliked each other. Calling Hitler the 'little corporal', the President refused him any part in government.

Meanwhile, support for the Nazi Party continued to grow. Industry and the Army were filling the Party coffers.

The SA was giving Hitler problems however. They were becoming out of control. They numbered 60 000 and perpetrated acts of violence without Hitler's say so. The SA was beginning to see itself as a power beyond the party organization.

Hitler had to use his own bodyguard, the SS, commanded by Heinrich Himmler, to suppress a SA revolt. But the problem of the SA was to return.

In September 1931 Hitler's niece, Geily Raubal, shot herself. The nature of their relationship, and the cause of her suicide, is shrouded in controversy. It is probable that Hitler loved her more than an uncle loves her niece. In any case he was extremely depressed after her death.

But now Hitler threw himself into the campaign for the 1932 presidential elections. At 87 Hindenburg was tired. He wanted to retire. Naturally Hitler sought the post for himself.

Bruning needed Hindenburg, and wanted to extend his term. He also needed Hitler to persuade Hindenburg to stay on.

Hitler would not give that support. Reluctantly, Hindenburg agreed to stand again.

On March 13 1932 Hitler received thirty per cent of the vote for President. But Hindenburg received forty – nine per cent.

A majority was required, and there had to be a second election. Hindenburg won his majority.

Bruning now acted swiftly. The SA had been growing at prodigious speed – in 1932 it numbered 400 000. He advised the President to issue a decree banning both the SA and the SS.

Hitler however, was not unduly worried. He knew that Bruning was desperate. The Republic was on the verge of collapse and that opportunity would soon come his way.

Opportunity came in the form of Kurt von Schleicher, an ambitious general who believed, like Hitler, that Germany could only be saved by a dictatorship.

Schleicher was against the SA ban, declaring that the SA was only arming itself against a potential Socialist coup. He saw an opportunity to join forces with the Nazis to gain power for himself.

Schleicher agreed to have the ban lifted and new elections called in return for Hitler's support in the formation of a conservative government that would not include Bruning.

Schleicher's intrigues succeeding in separating Hindenburg from the two men resisting Hitler: Chancellor Bruning and the presidential aide General Wilhelm Groener.

Hindenburg appointed the aristocrat Franz von Papen to the chancellorship. Papen was Schleicher's puppet. Hitler agreed to back Papen.

On June 14 the President dissolved the Reichstag and ordered a general election.

On June 15 the ban on the SA and SS was lifted. Schleicher and Papen had given back to Hitler the very tools he needed.

Immediately the SA was in the streets of Berlin, assaulting opponents and chanting 'blood must flow! Let's smash up … that goddamned Jewish Republic.' Outright war broke out between Nazis and Communists throughout Germany.

Papen declared martial law.

The general election in July gave the Nazis 37 per cent of the vote. They now had 203 seats in the Reichstag. It was now the largest party, and Hitler felt sure Schleicher would have to make him Chancellor.

Beside the Chancellorship, he demanded that the Reichstag pass an act making Germany a dictatorship. In addition Hitler was control the Ministry of the Interior, a new Ministry of Propaganda, and control of the state of Prussia, the largest and most powerful of the German states.

Schleicher prevaricated.

Even as the SA massed in Berlin in anticipation of Hitler's appointment, Hindenburg intervened. He would not have Hitler as Chancellor. He distrusted the upstart Austrian corporal and despised the thuggery of the SA.

Hitler reacted hysterically. Spewing venom, he threatened to let the SA loose on Germany if he did not get the chancellorship.

Stunned, Schleicher and Papen sought Hindenburg's help. Hitler was called to the presidential palace and received a reprimand from the old president himself.

Hitler calmed himself and backed down. His time would come.

On September 12 the Nazi element in Reichstag, presided over by Herman Goring, forced a successful motion of no confidence in the Chancellor.

Knowing, however, that he would not survive the vote, Papen advised the President to yet again call an election.

The Nazis were not expecting this, and were unprepared. They had believed that the chancellorship would be given to them on a plate.

There were signs that public support for the Nazi Party was waning. The SA in particular alienated many voters. Others were outraged by Hitler's behavior toward their president.

On November 6 the Nazis lost 34 seats. Power was slipping from their grasp.

Nevertheless Papen had to inform Hindenburg that he was unable to form a workable government. He resigned.

Immediately Hitler demanded the chancellorship again. Again Hindenburg refused. But he now realized that the government could not survive without Hitler. He asked him if he would co-operate in a coalition.

Now it was Hitler who held all the cards. He refused.

The machinery of government had by now grounded to a halt. Hindenburg had to do something. Papen suggested that he be made Chancellor with dictatorial powers. In other words, he would rule without the Reichstag.

Schleicher disagreed, wanting power for himself. He promised he could form a government if he were appointed Chancellor. He told Hindenburg that he could bring a number of Nazi deputies over.

Hindenburg wanted Papen. He would not trust the Nazis, and believed Schleicher deluded himself in believing that they could be controlled. Nevertheless Schleicher had the Army on his side.

Tears rolling down the old general's eyes, Hindenburg told Papen he had to appoint his rival in order to avoid civil war.

The new chancellor assumed office on December 2 1932. Immediately he executed his plan to split the Nazi vote in the Reichstag.

He offered the vice-chancellorship and the state of Prussia to Hitler's close associate Gregor Strasser.

Strasser found the offer attractive, and did not deny it when Hitler, Goring and Goebbels confronted him. He told them that the Nazis must co-operate with Schleicher's government.

When Strasser resigned from the Nazi Party Hitler reeled. Strasser had been a founding member of the Nazi Party. It seemed that Hitler's opportunity to rule Germany was slipping away.

Hitler went through a period of deep depression.

But the New Year brought in fresh hopes for the Nazis. Papen, eager to revenge himself on Schleicher, with the backing of industry and the banks, which wanted Hitler in, agreed to a government led by Hitler as Chancellor, and himself as Vice-Chancellor.

In desperation Schleicher begged Hindenburg to use his emergency powers yet again and dissolve the Reichstag. The tired old general had too much respect for the institutions of government, and refused.

Hindenburg loved his country, and had striven to protect Germany from chaos. But he had exhausted his power and endurance. On January 30 1933 he called Adolf Hitler to the presidential palace and appointed him Chancellor of Germany. The President could scarcely look at him.

'We have done it!' crowed Hitler.

He was cheered in the streets.

Chancellor

There were only two other Nazis in the new cabinet. One of them, Herman Goring, was Minister for Prussia.

Papen as Vice-Chancellor believed he could contain Hitler, who had no experience of running a country. He saw Hitler's appointment as part of a grand plan to restore aristocratic government to Germany, as it had been before World War I.

The Nazis would not form any part of that future government. They were merely a stepping stone.

But he had severely underestimated Hitler. One who had not was Erich Ludendorff,

Hitler's one time supporter in the 1923 Munich putsch.

'This evil man will plunge Germany into the abyss' he told Hindenburg.

Hitler did not bide his time. On his first day as Chancellor he persuaded Hindenburg to dissolve the Reichstag yet again.

He had refused this request to Schleicher only days before. Hitler wanted an enabling act that would give absolute power to the government. This could only be achieved if the Nazis had an absolutely majority in the Reichstag. Hindenburg reluctantly agreed.

In the meantime Hitler, Goring and Goebbels immediately set out to control state institutions and destroy potential opposition. The state Police was augmented with 50 000 members of the SA and SS. They raided Communist headquarters in Berlin and arrested all 4000 members.

The Nazi leadership then devised a plot to burn down the Reichstag building. It could use its destruction to declare a state of emergency and assume absolute powers.

A Dutch Communist by the name of Marinus van der Libbe had been in Berlin looking to start a revolt.

Libbe broke in the Reichstag building on February 27. By an extraordinary coincidence – if it was – SA Stormtroopers were already in the building with the same purpose. It appears they knew Libbe and may even have encouraged him.

Whatever the relationship between the Nazis and Libbe, the young man served their purposes well.

Hitler did not even feign outrage. He declared to a reporter that the fire was 'the beginning of a great epoch in German history.'

Hitler demanded, and received, emergency powers from Hindenburg, a confused, tired and jaded old man. The SA began to round up truckloads of Communists, Social Democrats, liberals and other opponents of the Nazis.

Fifty-one were killed. Others were tortured or imprisoned. The man responsible for the operation, Herman Goring, declared 'I do not have to worry about justice. My mission is only to destroy and exterminate.'

The first bloodletting had begun.

Elections were held on March 5 1933. Still the German people would not give Hitler his majority. The Nazis obtained 44 per cent of the vote.

Nevertheless Hitler presented his Enabling Bill before the Reichstag. He argued that he needed it to give him powers to reform the economy and promote friendly relations with France, Russia and the United Kingdom.

He would use his new powers sparingly, he said.

Even as the Reichstag considered the Bill, members of the SA browbeat the deputies with cries of 'we want the bill – or fire and murder.'

One man, Otto Wells, leader of the Social Democrats rose to defy Hitler. Hitler raged at him. 'Your death knell has sounded!' he proclaimed.

The Enabling Bill passed 484 to 84. The Social Democrats were the only ones to vote against it. Many of them would pay with their lives. And so the Republic voted itself out of existence.

Many Germans, including much of the intelligentsia, left Germany. As many stayed, believing that Hitler would be their savior.

Libbe was beheaded.

It Begins

The Nazis now began to implement their program. They would completely destroy what they saw as a liberal, corrupt, weak Germany and re-create it in their own image.

The first to feel their wrath were the Jews. Just a week after the passage of the Enabling Act, Hitler announced a national boycott of Jewish places of business.

On April 1 SA operatives were posted at Jewish establishments, most of which were closed for the Sabbath. At the same time Joseph Goebbels, a man who had written 'propaganda has absolutely nothing to do with the truth', railed against 'the atrocities of world Jewry.'

By the end of the year Jews were forbidden from holding public office, from the arts and entertainment industries and from journalism. Jewish children were being barred from state-run schools.

Students burnt Jewish and other 'UnGerman' books with the encouragement of Goebbels. Einstein, Freud, Hemingway, Proust, London, Marx – the works of these and many more were consigned to the flames with youthful zeal.

Some 20 000 volumes were destroyed. University professors; afraid, opportunistic or genuinely enthusiastic, pledged allegiance to the ideals of Aryanism. Those who did not were sacked.

In attacking the intelligentsia Hitler had savagely removed anyone who could be a focus of opposition.

That is, almost anyone. By the beginning of 1934 Hitler was ready to turn his attention to the problem of the SA.

The SA had been instrumental in bringing Hitler to power, but it had outlived its purpose.

Hitler now had the Army. Moreover, he needed the Army. It supported him, but for how long? It perceived the SA as a potential rival.

The SA itself viewed itself as having a role beyond Adolf Hitler. In 1934 it talked of a second Nazi revolution, one that would complete the work of 1933. It talked of a complete redistribution of wealth and property.

When the SA leader Ernst Rohm learned that Hitler wish to diminish the role of the SA, he denounced Hitler as a traitor, and declared publicly that 'the SA is the National Socialist Revolution!'

Tensions between Hitler and the SA threatened the new regime. Papen the Vice-Chancellor became involved. Even Hindenburg, feeling his power again and perhaps seeing a chance to rid Germany of the 'little corporal', threatened to bring the Army in.

On June 30 Hitler personally arrested Rohm. A few hours later he ordered Goring to execute a ruthless purge.

Members of the Gestapo, Hitler's secret police, and Himmler's SS, searched out enemies and potential enemies of Hitler and savagely murdered them.

The leaders of the SA, plus other 'unwanted persons' were on the execution list. Among the dead were Gregor Strasser, the ex-Chancellor Schleicher, and from the Beer Hall Putsch days, 73 year old Gustav von Kahr.

Rohm himself was shot, after refusing to shoot himself.

The total number slaughtered in the 72 hour long purge will probably never be known. It may be as high as a 1000. Less than half were SA leaders. Hitler, Goring, Goebbels and Himmler were settling old scores.

From the presidential palace the old, ailing general congratulated Hitler. He had been told the threat of revolt was imminent and that the measures had been legally sanctioned.

The Army likewise applauded the Chancellor.

This orgy of bloodletting has gone down in history as the Night of the Long Knives.

Even now Hitler was not absolutely secure. There remained one person who barred his way, and that was the President, Paul von Hindenburg.

The President was close to death and everyone knew it. Papen, who had narrowly escaped the purge with his life, saw one last chance of restoring the old aristocratic regime that he and other conservatives longed for.

He persuaded the President to restore the monarchy, but Hindenburg later decided to instead present a personal request to Hitler.

Surely Hindenburg realized that Hitler would dismiss a restoration with derision. After all, Hitler held the Kaiser as one of the leaders responsible for the betrayal of Germany in 1918. Perhaps the worn out president was simply going through the motions.

At about 9 am on August 2 1934 Hindenburg died. He had been the last link with the old order.

Without even proclaiming a period of mourning, Hitler proclaimed a new law combining the office of President and Chancellor.

Every member of the German military was now required to swear the Oath of Allegiance to Hitler personally.

Shortly after, a national plebiscite approve of Hitler's actions.

Fuhrer

Hitler now used his title as leader of the Party - title Fuhrer (leader) – in his capacity as Head of State. There was now no distinction between State and Party.

He renewed his attack on the Jews. In September 1935 he enacted the Nuremburg Laws, forbidding marriage and sexual relations between Aryans and Jews.

Anti-Jewish demonstrations and violence was permitted and encouraged across Germany. Much of the violence came from the SA and SS. However the civilian population frequently joined in.

World reaction stayed Hitler's hand and, for now, he would not go beyond the Nuremburg Laws.

But he only cared about world reaction insofar as he needed credibility to further another of the Party's goals – repudiating the Treaty of Versailles.

In 1935 Hitler announced to the world that he would reintroduce conscription, and raise the size of the Army from 1000 000 to 550 000.

This was a clear violation of Versailles.

But the powers did nothing. France was politically divided and Britain was economically wounded. Both countries breathed a sigh of relief when Hitler assured them that he only wanted peace.

On March 7 1936 Hitler sent German troops into the German Rhineland. The Treaty had declared this a military free zone.

The German force was miniscule – only 19 battalions. The French began massing thousands of troops on the Rhineland border.

It was a tense situation. The German High Command knew that if the French engaged the German forces Germany could not win. The occupying troops were ordered to retreat if the French moved.

Yet neither France nor Britain acted. Britain had no stomach for war, and neither did the French generals.

Hitler's gamble had paid off. He had effectively torn up the Treaty of Versailles.

Looking back from our own time, it seems incredible that France and Britain did not take a relatively easy step to check Hitler's ambitions.

We must remember however, that the world of 1936 had emerged from a frightful war, the likes of which had never been experienced before. A whole generation had been slaughtered, and so it was understandable that the peoples of Europe wish to avoid another war.

This is not to say that the politics of appeasement and the failure to check the Nazis cannot be criticized, even in the context of its own time.

After the success in the Rhineland Hitler began secret preparations for war, as outlined in Mein Kampf, which as we have said were plain for all to read. Germany would knock out France, and then turn its attention to Russia.

But certain actions were necessary before war could be considered.

In 1938 Hitler sought an Anschluss (union) with Austria. This had been forbidden by the terms of Versailles. Hitler handed the Austrian Chancellor, Kurt von Schuschnigg, and ultimatum demanding the appointment of Nazis to top government positions and the assimilation of Austria's economy into Germany's.

When Austria refused, Germany invaded Austria on March 12. Not a short was fired. Most Austrians greeted the soldiers as liberating heroes.

Once again, Britain and France did nothing.

Czechoslovakia was next on Hitler's list. Created after the First World War, this country was made up of Slav Czechs and Slovaks.

There were also ethnic Germans living in the borderlands of Czech Bohemia. Hitler now demanded that these parts, called the Sudentenland, become German.

This time Britain and France intervened. On September 15 1938 Neville Chamberlain, the Prime Minister of Great Britain, flew to Munich for talks with Hitler.

Chamberlain had been informed by a group of dissident German generals that Hitler planned to invade Czechoslovakia. However, Chamberlain distrusted the German military and was intent on his own peace plan.

After an apparently cordial meeting Chamberlain returned to London. He told his colleagues that Hitler was a man who could be trusted.

Britain, France and Czechoslovakia agreed to the cession of the Sudetenland in return for a guarantee of peace.

However, on September 22 Hitler personally told Chamberlain that Germany would take all of Czechoslovakia.

Chamberlain realized he had been duped. France began mobilizing. The British Fleet began preparations to put out to sea. It seemed war was inevitable.

But Germany was still not ready for all-out war, and Hitler agreed to further talks.

A meeting was scheduled in Munich again. This time the French premier, Daladier, and Mussolini joined Hitler and Chamberlain.

The Czech deputation was not allowed to participate.

Backed by Mussolini, Hitler again demanded the Sudetenland. France and Britain agreed without a fight. An agreement was signed on September 30.

Chamberlain returned triumphant, famously declaring 'peace for our time'. In Britain, Winston Churchill alone declared Munich 'an unmitigated defeat.'

Just two days after the ink from the signatures had dried, German troops occupied the Sudetenland. Czechoslovakia offered no resistance.

Meanwhile, in Germany, what little moderation that existed within the Nazi Party could no longer contain anti-Semitic extremism.

The Kristallnacht ('Night of Broken Glass') from the ninth to the tenth of September 1938 was a deliberate, coordinated pogrom that saw the murder of hundreds of Jews and the arrest of 30 000.

Homes, hospitals, schools and synagogues were burnt. Stores and businesses were ransacked. The streets were littered with the glass that gave the horrific event its name.

A German diplomat Ernst vom Rath had been shot by a Polish Jew, Herschel Grynzspan in Paris. Grynzspan had been expelled from Germany in October, along with 17000 Jews of Polish origin. Rath later died of his wounds.

Hitler and Goebbels deliberately used the incident to incite the German people against the Jews. Both the SA and civilians participated.

The world was horrified, but did nothing.

Herschel later fell into the hands of the Gestapo and disappeared without trace.

On March 14 1939 Hitler summoned Hacha, the President of Czechoslovakia, to Berlin. Without any presence of diplomatic courtesy he gave Hacha an ultimatum: surrender peacefully or see his nation destroyed.

Hacha was shocked. He collapsed and was revived by Hitler's own doctor. Pale and shaken, he telephoned his government and advised it not to resist the German invasion.

Two hours later the invasion began. German troops met almost no resistance.

In Britain Chamberlain was intent on keeping the peace, declaring that Britain was not bound to come to Czechoslovakia's aid. But he was alone in the House of Commons. MPs demanded that the politics of appeasement stop.

Chamberlain changed tack. He denounced Hitler's violation of the Munich Agreement, and together with France guaranteed the territorial integrity of Poland.

Poland was Germany's next target. The Treaty of Versailles had given Poland a large part of eastern Prussia, as well as the 'Polish Corridor', a strip of land giving Poland access to the Baltic Sea.

The likelihood of a conflict over Poland became stronger after the signing of a non-aggression pact between Germany and the Soviet Union of August 23 1939.

This agreement, engineered by Joachim von Ribbentrop, the German Foreign Minister, laid down that Germany and Russia would not fight one another. This was essential to Hitler if he was to destroy France.

Secret clauses of the agreement divided Poland between Germany and Russia and let

Estonia, Latvia and Finland fall into Russia's sphere of influence.

Now Hitler believed himself ready for war. Germany had been steadily re-arming. He called his generals together and told them to be ready. 'Close your hearts to pity!' he told them. They listened in silence.

Hitler explained the plan for starting a war with Poland. It involved the SS faking attacks of 'Polish' troops on Germans. The invasion would begin on August 26 1939.

Two events happened to stall the plan. Britain and Poland signed a treaty of mutual assistance, and Mussolini told Hitler that Italy was not prepared for war.

Hitler did not want to go to war with Britain. After all, the English were of Germanic origin. He told Halifax, the British Foreign Secretary, that he wanted an understanding with Britain.

Britain responded that it was anxious to keep the peace. The British agreed to persuade Poland to negotiate with Hitler.

But Hitler was not interested in negotiation. His offer was merely a delaying tactic.

At 10 am on September 1 1939 Hitler told the Reichstag, still sitting but utterly powerless, that German troops crossed the Polish border at dawn.

Around the same time, in accordance with the secret protocols of the German-Russian Pact, Soviet troops invaded eastern Poland.

At 9pm that night British Ambassador Henderson presented a note demanding that German troops withdraw from Poland immediately. An hour later the French ambassador demanded likewise.

Mussolini intervened and suggested the powers negotiate. The British replied that there would be no negotiation.

Hitler was non-plussed that Britain had finally drawn a line in the sand. He appears to have not expected war with Britain.

When Ribbentrop showed him the ultimatum from Britain, Hitler, uncharacteristically indecisive, asked his foreign minister 'what now?'

Hitler decided he could not back down and risk humiliation. He did not respond to the ultimatums.

At 11am on September 2 the British ultimatum expired. Europe had been at peace for less than 25 years.

War

With the bulk of the German Army occupied in Poland, the large French Army enjoyed a numerical advantage in the west. Moreover, the French/German border was protected by a line of near-impregnable forts known as the Maginot Line, named after a French minister of war.

A French offensive into the industrial Rhineland would likely have crippled German industry and forced troops to withdraw from Poland.

Instead the French remained, with their British allies, behind the Maginot Line. Many of their generals had fought in World War I and remembered the appalling slaughter.

Huge armies ground against each other, bleeding hundreds of thousands of men for only a few miles advance.

But warfare had changed since then, as they were to discover to their cost.

But if French generals were cautious, French politicians were even more so. The government simply lacked the leadership for decisive action.

Hitler could scarcely believe his luck. Every major decision on the road to war had been a gamble: the Rhineland; Austria; Czechoslovakia. And all had paid off. It seemed now that Poland might be a triumph too. Surely he must have thought he was a child of destiny.

With Poland crushed in just 27 days, Hitler offered an olive branch to Britain and France in a speech he made before the Reichstag on October 6.

'Germany has no further claims against France', he said. He declared that he sought, and had ever sought, an understanding with Britain.

Daladier, on behalf of the French demanded certain guarantees. Chamberlain's reply was sterner. He had now abandoned the role of peace-maker on any terms. He denounced Hitler's speech in the House of Commons, commenting that it made no mention of Poland.

Goebbels and his propaganda machine seized on Chamberlain's remarks as proof that it was Britain, not Germany that desired war.

On October 10, ignoring the cautionary advice of the High Command, he ordered his generals to invade France, Belgium and the Netherlands.

Some senior generals, including Walther von Brauchitsch and Franz Halder, considered removing Hitler from power to avoid what they were convinced would be a military disaster.

The idea of a coup was dropped, as the generals could not rely on the loyalty of junior officers. Nevertheless Hitler did delay the invasion.

What followed was a strange lull in military activity. This period from the fall of Poland in September 1939 to the invasion of France in May 1940 has been called the Phoney War.

During this time Hitler did invade Norway and Denmark, and the British launched a failed defense of Norway. But the French and British remained behind the Maginot Line.

These months however were also disadvantageous to Hitler. Britain managed to establish a naval blockade of German shipping lanes.

The attack on France in earnest began at last on May 10 1940.

The Battle of France, as the invasion has been called, introduced the Allies to a new kind of warfare.

The Germans called it blitzkrieg, 'lightning war.' Tanks broke through enemy lines, aided by heavy concentrations of artillery and supported by aircraft.

Swift and decisive, these attacks avoided the heavy casualties of World War I.

In just six weeks Netherlands, Belgium, and then France, succumbed to the German Army.

Hitler was elated, but surprised. Film footage showing Hitler dancing a jig when he received news of the French surrender was edited by the Allies for propaganda purposes. In the original he is actually stepping back in shock.

The French leadership was indecisive, both on the battlefield and in Paris. Italy joined the invasion in June 1940. The government panicked and fled the capital.

Unable to procure an agreement on an armistice, the President, Albert Lebrun, resigned. He was replaced by Phillipe Petain, a Marshal of France and hero of the First World War I.

The task of surrendering fell to Petain. Hitler arranged the capitulation to take place on the very train, near Compiegne, where Germany surrendered on November 11 1918.

On June 21 1940 Hitler began the armistice negotiations, but soon left in calculated disdain for the French deputation. He left proceedings to his Chief of Staff Wilhelm Keitel.

France had to surrender Alsace-Lorraine. Northern France was to be occupied by German troops.

Hitler's goals, as described in Mein Kampf, were being achieved with frightening speed. National Socialism was triumphant, the Jews were oppressed, and the Treaty of Versailles was torn up. Now Alsace-Lorraine had been restored to Germany and France was humiliated. Hitler must have thought he was a god.

But Hitler now made a grave mistake. He was certain Britain would now negotiate a peace. He had no claims against Britain and had never desired war with the British people.

The new Prime Minister of the United Kingdom, Winston Churchill, was resolute. There would be no peace. He believed, correctly, that Hitler had to conquer Britain or lose the war.

Hitler could now tell the German people that it was Churchill and not himself who was continuing the war.

To the great consternation of his generals Hitler ordered a plan to be drawn up for the invasion of Britain.

A sea-borne invasion was almost impossible, on account of the undoubted superiority of the Royal Navy.

The German High Command suggested an invasion might be possible by May 1941.

In the meantime Herman Goring, now Chief of the Luftwaffe or Air Force saw an opportunity of ingratiating himself with the

Fuhrer. He boasted that his planes could bring Britain to its knees.

The generals were doubtful but Hitler gave the go-ahead. The result was the famous Battle of Britain from July to October 1940.

Outnumbered and outgunned, the British and Allied Air Forces held off the Luftwaffe, and began bombing raids of their own over German soil, including Berlin.

The Battle of Britain was Hitler's first major defeat. The invasion of Britain had to be postponed indefinitely. He was furious.

Goring, who had declared that no English bombs would fall on Berlin, lost standing within the Nazi Party and with Hitler personally.

Yet Britain was powerless to launch a land attack against Germany, and so Hitler could turn his attention to his next target – Russia.

Hitler held Russia in derision. He believed the Slavs were untermenschen (subhuman). The proof of this was they were, according to him, governed by Jews. Hitler believed that Bolshevism was Jewish in origin. Hence the Communist regime of Russia was profoundly degenerate.

In addition to this, the German people needed their lebensraum (living space). The vast expanses of Russia were to be colonized by the Master Race.

Hitler's aim was not simply to defeat Russia as it had defeated France, but to annihilate it. Civilians were to be exterminated along with soldiers.

The generals were profoundly uneasy. They baulked at the killing of non-combatants. Nevertheless they felt bounden to Hitler and acquiesced.

The invasion of Russia, Operation Barbarossa (named after Frederick I Barbarossa, a medieval German emperor who had also attacked the Slavs) commenced on June 22 1941.

Hitler had made his second mistake. News of the invasion stunned the world. Russia was a vast country with wide open spaces, capable of raising hundreds of thousands of soldiers.

In 1813 Napoleon, one of the greatest generals Europe had ever seen, invaded with a vast army and utterly failed. His defeat led to his ultimate downfall.

Germans at home were disconcerted when they heard the news. One man remarked to his daughter 'Now we have lost the war!'

The worry at first seemed unwarranted. Hundreds of thousands of Russian soldiers- whole armies – reeled and surrendered before the German blitzkrieg, exactly as the Poles and French had done.

As Hitler had commanded, the Russian population was brutally pillaged and massacred as the German armies advanced.

Josef Stalin, the Russian leader, had been taken completely by surprise, despite receiving intelligence reports that an invasion was imminent. He was convinced that Hitler would only invade Russia after he had defeated Britain.

By the middle of 1941, with Germany armies poised to take the important Baltic city of Leningrad (now called St Petersburg), it seemed that Russia was about to surrender.

But it did not. The Russians continued to fight. The Red (Soviet) Army was mobilizing to full strength – some 3 million men.

Resistance, both military and civilian, was stiffening against the Germans.

The brutal destruction and killing ordered by Hitler was not having its desired effect. It was in fact inflaming opposition.

Hitler's generals saw one chance to bring Russia to its knees. The capital, Moscow, had to be taken, before the summer was over and the terrible Russian Winter began to creep in.

Hitler, however, dismissed a summer offensive against Moscow in favor of an attack on Leningrad.

Hitler felt the fall of Leningrad, named after Lenin, the mastermind of the Russian

Bolshevik revolution, would break Russian morale and cause the Soviets to capitulate.

In October 1941, sensing the fall of Leningrad, and sure that Moscow would follow; Hitler announced victory to the German people.

But when the Russian winter, named 'General Winter' by a previous invader, Napoleon, the Germans had ground to a halt.

The soldiers were now cold, frostbitten and lacking supplies. Vehicles seized up and machine guns jammed. Corpses of German soldiers lay stiff in the deep snow.

From October to January the Germans attacked Moscow and lost. It was the first major defeat of a German army since the war began. The defeat was ultimately to lose them the war.

The generals now told Hitler that the invasion of Russia had failed and that the troops should retreat to defensive positions.

Hitler would not believe that destiny had abandoned him. With his characteristic disregard for human life he refused to allow the German forces to retreat.

The German reversal was about to be compounded.

On June 7 1941 Japan attacked Pearl Harbor. Germany had an alliance with Japan, and, although the terms of that alliance did not require it Hitler declared war on the United States.

The declaration of war was probably Hitler's greatest error. He made the decision entirely on his own.

It seems he did not seriously consider the possibility that the United States would attack Germany before dealing with Japan.

Unlike the leaders in the United Kingdom, Russia and the United States, he refused to take counsel. Instead he relied upon his own infallibility as a man destined for glory.

He had lost the chance for victory in Russia. Britain was secure from invasion. Now the United States was in the war, supplying its allies with much needed resources and reinforcements.

In 1942 United States forces began landing in North Africa, where Germany and its ally Italy was fighting British forces under Rommel.

The Germans and Italians were swiftly driven out of Africa. Moreover the Allies launched an invasion of Italy in July 1943. Mussolini's troops could not effectively resist, and so Hitler had to transfer forces from the Eastern Front to assist.

Hitler was furious at having to divert resources to its weaker ally.

Hitler's master plan was now unravelling at a frantic and uncontrollable pace.

The Final Solution

On January 20 1942 a small group of Nazi administrators met at the Wannsee Vilsa in Berlin at the direction of Reinhard Heydrich, head of the SA and Chief of Police.

Hitler was not present, though he knew of the group's existence and purpose.

That purpose was to implement a permanent solution to the 'problem' of the Jews. Heydrich told the meeting that there were 11 million Jews in Europe. They were to be rounded up and transported to SS ghettos in Poland.

In those concentration camps many would perish through malnutrition and ill treatment.

But this would not be enough. A number of special camps would have to be constructed where the inmates would be gassed to death. Once they were operational the trains carrying Jews would bypass the ghettos and go directly to the gas chambers.

Historians have asked if this order came directly from Hitler. There is no direct evidence that he explicitly ordered the Holocaust, or even publicly acknowledged it.

What they do know is that Hitler gave a directive to Goring in 1939 to the effect that the solution to the Jewish 'problem' had to include the 'complete removal of the Jews.'

Goring passed this onto Heydrich in 1941, telling him that he should make 'all necessary preparations with regard to organizational, practical and financial aspects for an overall solution to the Jewish question.'

So while a chain of directives leading to the holocaust can be traced to Hitler it seems he was careful not to explicitly order it. However he would make a veiled reference to the Holocaust in his last hours.

It beggars belief to suggest that Hitler did not know what he was asking his subordinates to do. He must have been aware of what Heydrich was doing and certainly made no attempt to stop it. The Final Solution is entirely consistent with everything Hitler stood for and yet he seems not to have taken ownership of it.

He proudly took responsibility for every other action of the Party, however ruthless it was. Could it be that he could not hold himself accountable for the ultimate logical consequence of everything he ever stood for?

In August 1944 Adolf Eichmann, one of the organizers of the Holocaust, reported that 4 million Jews had been gassed and 2 million shot. One and half million of these were children.

News of the murders leaked to the outside world, but there was little reaction. A few newspapers published reports. Some politicians made speeches.

It is to be wondered why there was no stronger response. Perhaps people were just so weary of horror that these fresh atrocities could rouse no further outrage. Or perhaps there was an unwillingness to believe that such things could happen.

In addition to the Jews other persons considered unfit to live also perished, including Poles, Russians and other Slavs, the physically and mentally disabled (Aryans included), homosexuals, gypsies, Freemasons, Communist and Jehovah's Witnesses

The End

On July 22 1944 a group of German generals
including Claus von Stauffenburg and
Ludwig Beck initiated a plot to kill Hitler
and take over the government

Stauffenburg visited Wolf's Lair, the Fuhrer's
HQ in East Prussia and left a briefcase
containing a bomb. The bomb was set to
explode with Hitler and a number of top-
ranking generals present.

Stauffenburg and his allies were alarmed
that Hitler had taken personal day to day
command of military operations. He was
making serious mistakes and errors of
judgement.

The Russians were retaking their soil and would soon be at the Polish border. Mussolini's regime had crumbled (Mussolini remained, but now as a German puppet). The Allies controlled Rome and were moving north toward Germany.

After Hitler's death Stauffenburg would stage a coup in Berlin and approach the Allies to seek peace.

The plot failed. The bomb went off at 12.42 pm. The explosion killed 4 people and injured 23, but Hitler himself escaped with only minor injuries. An officer had unwittingly moved the briefcase away from Hitler.

Nevertheless did not try to ascertain whether Hitler was dead or not. Instead he flew to Berlin to announce the Fuhrer's demise.

Yet the conspirators lost their nerve, not knowing if Hitler was truly dead. This hesitation was to cost them and hundreds of others their lives.

The coup proceeded half-heartedly until it was clear that Hitler was alive. The coup collapsed and Remer, commander of the troops guarding the Propaganda Ministry in Berlin, resecured the capital.

Stauffenburg and several others were executed. Beck was arrested and shot after an unsuccessful suicide attempt.

Ironically the plot galvanized Hitler at a time when everything was turning against him. He was convinced that he had been spared to fulfil the destiny of the German people.

A rejuvenated Hitler took a terrible revenge. Hundreds, including many not involved in the plot, were executed. Others committed suicide to escape retribution. The purge was still going on when Soviet troops crossed the German border in February 1945.

After the plot Hitler was highly suspicious of his generals. He never trusted their judgement again, preferring his own counsel. This was to have the direst consequences.

In July 1943 the hapless citizens of Hamburg experienced a horrific event. Bombing from Allied planes had created a tornado-like fire storm that consumed the city. Children were swept from their parents' arms into the fire. People threw themselves into the Elbe River, but to no avail. The water was scalding and the air scorched their throats.

Hitler did not care for the sufferings of the German people. The more events turned against him the more he was convinced that his generals and his people were betraying him.

In his mind he could not possibly be the cause. Had not his instincts been correct in every stage of his career? Had not providence preserved him on July 20? Surely victory would still be his.

He did what any person who refuses to see reality does. He shut it out.

After the attempted coup he decimated what remained of the old aristocratic order; in the military, in the diplomatic corps, in politics and administration. He surrounded himself with people who would not question his increasingly flawed and ego-driven judgement.

Ironically, at the very time he assumed the greatest personal power he also became the most vulnerable. He had eliminated any rational influence that might have moderated what was to come.

His health began to decline. The bomb had in fact affected him on July 20. His right eardrum was ruptured and his balance was impaired.

Doctors prescribed a cocktail of drugs which produced deleterious side effects. He experienced severe insomnia. His once sharp mind addled. Often he had to be reminded who he was speaking to.

Hitler could become quite charming and disarming but now his language was increasingly intemperate, his violent outbursts more frequent. He refused to believe anyone, ignoring bad reports of band denouncing inevitable failures as acts of betrayal.

Incredibly, there were those who still revered him and were convinced that he would lead Germany to victory.

In the summer of 1944 Allied forces landed in Normandy. They liberated France and advanced toward the Rhine.

Despite these setbacks Hitler saw a chance to deal a blow that might set the Allied advance back weeks, maybe even months.

The Allies had overstretched themselves. They needed time to regroup and resupply. The old Hitler, willing to place his fortunes on a risk, resurfaced and ordered the last German offensive of the war.

Hitler believed that he could split the US forces and crush the British/Canadian forces, thus gaining time to transfer men to the east and thwart the imminent Soviet invasion of Germany.

In order to do this he had to take troops away from the Eastern Front. If he failed, Germany was lost on both fronts.

His generals were incredulous. They simply did not have the manpower. The Fuhrer reminded them of the exploits of Frederick the Great of Prussia who had likewise fought and won against seemingly insurmountable odds.

We know this last offensive as the Battle of the Bulge, on account of the bulge created in the front by the German advance.

For a time the attack seemed to be succeeding. It placed real pressure on the US troops. However the Germans achieved none of their objectives, and when the US 101st Airborne Division famously held the

Belgian town of Bastogne the offensive had been halted.

The German generals now asked Hitler to revise the plan. He refused them as he had refused them in Russia.

For the first the word armistice was mentioned, but not by Hitler. Goring advised the Fuhrer to seek terms from the Allies.

Hitler exploded in rage. The generals were cowards, he said. He told Goring he would be shot if he went to the Allied.

No terms could have been negotiated in any case. The principal leaders of the Allied powers: Roosevelt, Churchill and Stalin, had already agreed not to make a separate peace, and that they would only accept an unconditional surrender.

The British and Americans were now positioning themselves for an invasion of Germany itself. In the east the Soviets had delivered a crushing defeat and were doing likewise.

Still Hitler refused to admit that he had made a mistake. Still he believed in his own personal infallibility. He believed he was Germany's destiny.

In his mind the only way to rationalize these defeats was to believe that he had been betrayed. The generals were weak and cowardly. The people were weak. Even his close associates were weak. Everybody had failed except him.

The German people were to discover that Hitler's contempt for life included their own.

The Battle of the Bulge sent Hitler into a state of deep despair. He retired to a bunker near the Reich Chancellery building in Berlin. There he isolated himself with his personal staff and closest associates, including his mistress Eva Braun.

He did not speak to his people, nor offer them any words of comfort.

The Soviet forces approaching Berlin raped, murdered and pillaged. Whole families killed themselves rather than suffer Soviet occupation.

Hitler ordered his troops to stand and die rather than give ground to the invading troops. Deserters were shot.

Sixteen year old boys were recruited and placed in the front lines. Hitler Youth boys, some as young as ten, along with old men, were entrusted with the defense of Berlin.

On March 19 1945 Hitler ordered the destruction of what remained of the German economy and infrastructure – industries, farms, railways, mines, bridges, food – everything. He would not give an inch to Allies.

He justified this to Albert Speer, Minister of Armaments. The survivors would be the weakest, he said, and thus undeserving of any good.

He thus turned upon the very people that had supposedly justified anything he had ever done.

Speer rescinded as much of the order as he could. Most of the remaining infrastructure was saved.

In his bunker Hitler was but a shadow of his former self. He was stooped low. He was pale. When walking he propped himself up against furniture or the walls.

He still raged during military conferences. He would give orders for units that no longer existed and scream at the imbecility of officers who dared to contradict him. Even now he refused to accept the reality of what was happening. He still talked of counterattack and victory.

Meanwhile Allied forces were entering the concentration camps, seeing piles of corpses and the emaciated living, walking as if they were dead.

In April American troops were only 50 miles from Berlin.

On April 22 Hitler berated his generals. He denounced the 'universal treason' that had denied him his destiny.' The war is lost!' he cried. Now he finally realized the inevitable, but still would not accept any responsibility.

Some in Hitler's circle who still believed in him urged him to leave the bunker and go to his mountain retreat at Berchtesgaden on the Austrian border. German forces still held out there.

He refused. He could not risk being captured. He did however give permission for anyone who wished to leave to do so.

'I will fight as long as long as I have a single soldier,' he said. 'When the last soldier deserts me I will shoot myself.'

But Hitler's destruction was not yet complete. The two men most loyal to him, Goring and Himmler, were both shocked and appalled by Hitler's resignation to fate.

Goring sent a telegram to the bunker asking Hitler if he should assume the leadership. Hitler accused Goring of treason, and stripped him of his position and titles.

In the meantime Himmler contact Count Berhadotte, of the Swedish Red Cross, and asked him to mediate with the General Eisenhower, commander of the Allied forces in the west. He suggested that they might join with Germany in defeating Russia. Himmler would, of course, lead Germany.

The notion was desperate and absurd, and went nowhere. As mentioned, the Allies had agreed on nothing less than total surrender from Germany, and the idea that a mass murderer like Himmler could ever be trusted was unthinkable.

Hitler raged like a madman. If anyone had been faithful to him, it was 'Faithful Heinrich.' Hitler ordered his execution. Since Himmler could not be found, his personal liaison officer, Fegelein, was shot instead.

By now the Red Army had broken the Berlin defenses. There was savage fighting in the streets, since Hitler had forbidden any units to surrender.

On April 29 he married Eva Braun in the bunker. Braun had known Hitler since the death of Geili Raubul. She had been neglected by Hitler, and had attempted to take her life twice during the time of their relationship.

Hitler saw himself as a chaste Germanic hero, married only to Germany. His sexuality remains a topic of debate, but he seems to have been genuinely fond of Eva.

After the wedding breakfast Hitler shut himself away with Traudl Junge, his personal secretary.

He dictated his will to Junge. He dismissed Goring and Himmler for the Nazi Party and appointed Admiral Karl Donitz President of the Reich and Goebbels as Chancellor. He was determined that the title Fuhrer would die with him.

He further declared his wish that he and his wife should shoot themselves, and their bodies be destroyed to prevent them being taken by the Russians.

In the will he blamed the war on the Jews. Facing his own death, he still would not accept any responsibility for the years of violence and slaughter that had brought his people to the verge of destruction.

His testament makes a veiled reference to the extermination of the Jews, stating that they were killed 'by humane means.'

Hitler's entourage began to abandon him to escape the Soviets.

The last military order Hitler gave was both astounding and bizarre. In a directive to the High Command he again exonerates himself from any responsibility for failure. He tells the generals it is they, not he, who have betrayed Germany. He cannot help them now.

At the same time he expresses a mind-boggling abandonment of any sense of reality. He directs High Command to conquer territory from the east for the

German people, for 'the efforts and sacrifices of the German people have been so great I cannot believe they have been in vain.'

Shortly after Hitler received word that his ally Mussolini had been executed by Italian partisans, along with his mistress.

Hitler handed out cyanide pills to his secretaries, assuming that they would wish to die with him. Even the animals were not to be spared. His favorite German shepherd, Blonde, was killed by cyanide.

Strangely, the mood in the bunker lightened. Members of Hitler's staff, civilian and military, danced and laughed and drank as the Red Army fired on positions just one block away.

On April 30 1945 Hitler received a military briefing. Afterward he had a meat-free lunch (he was a vegetarian).

He and Eva Braun then bade farewell to their entourage and retired to their private room. A few moments later, at 3.30 pm, a shot was heard.

Goebbels and Martin Bormann, a top-ranking Nazi official, entered the room. They found Hitler dead, shot in the temple with the pistol he had used in the Beer Hall Putsch in 1923. Braun was also dead. She had swallowed cyanide.

The two bodies were taken into the Reich Chancellery Garden, doused in gasoline and burnt. While they burnt Bormann and now Chancellor Goebbels gave the Nazi salute.

Goebbels was distraught. Of all Hitler's henchmen he had been the most fanatically devoted. He and his wife poisoned all six of their children. Then they poisoned themselves and were shot by an SS operative.

At 10 pm on May 1 it was announced by radio that Hitler had died 'fighting for Germany against Bolshevism.' By this time the Soviets had taken the Chancellery and were sifting through the remains of the Fuhrer, his wife and the Goebbels.

Admiral Donitiz, now President of the Reich, had of course no intention of continuing the struggle. But he did want to give the German people enough time to flee to the parts of Germany occupied by the Americans and British – this protecting them from the frightful Soviet retribution.

He stalled an armistice for as long as he could, which was not long. General Eisenhower refused to give Donitz the time he wanted. On May 7 1945, General Josef Jodl unconditionally surrendered the forces of the Reich to Eisenhower on behalf of Donitz.

The war in Europe was over.

Another Hitler?

When Jodl signed the surrender 54 000 000 people had perished in Europe. Most of them were civilians. Eleven million civilians were refugees, including 100 000 Jewish survivors from the concentration camps.

After the war the surviving leaders of Nazi Germany were put on trial in Nuremburg.

The evil mastermind of the Nazi regime had escaped having to personally answer the court for his crimes. Nevertheless, he was on trial.

The question was asked – how could human beings convince themselves and others that barbaric slaughter on a massive scale was justified?

How could violence and calculated murder be acceptable as a tool of policy?

Today we ask ourselves the same question, and it is not simply a question for Nazi Germany. It is a question for all time, the present day included.

The same prejudices and fears that lifted Hitler to power are still present now.

Antisemitism is still with us, and even appears to be on the rise. The Protocols of the Learned Elders of Zion is still widely read and quoted despite it being refuted as a forgery (and a bad one at that) time and time again.

The ISIS movement certainly exhibits Nazi-like behaviors, but radical intolerance is prevalent in cultures of western origin as well.

Nationalism is on the rise in the west, as elsewhere, fueled by the fear of immigrants, ethnic minorities, homosexuals, and others considered alien to 'authentic' culture.

Politics groups adhering to Fascist doctrine exist all across the world, even in the democracies that fought Hitler in the Second World War.

There are at least 8 Fascist parties active in the United Kingdom. In the United States the American Freedom Party professes to be 'a political party for White Americans' and warns against the corrupting influence of immigrants and homosexuals. The neo-Nazi party Russian National Unity openly displays the Swastika and calls for the expulsion of all non- Russians.

We may dismiss these small groups as deluded and dangerous but practically harmless.

Perhaps so, but do they tap into a primal fear all people have? Are we not all, on some level, fearful of what we do not understand, of the foreigner, of the 'other'?

Perhaps when we consider how Hitler could have done what he did in Germany we should be asking questions closer to home. What primordial fears do we have?

Could some masterful demagogue take advantage of those fears, and create a world that would shield us from fear, but at the expense of others?

It is worth noting that although Hitler may have been psychopathic and deluded by self-aggrandizement, he was not clinically insane.

His thoughts were quite rational in the light of his ideas, though the premises of his philosophy were irrational. He followed his philosophy to its ultimate conclusion.

Fear and prejudice built Nazism. If we wish to ensure that it never returns we must strive to build a world built on tolerance and understanding. This means seeking truth rather than have demagogues tell us what truth is.

Josef Mengele Angel of Death

A Biography of Nazi Evil

Anna Revell

Introduction

Better known as the Angel of Death today Dr. Josef Mengele is best remembered for the series of grisly experiments and murders he carried out during the Holocaust.

Born in 1911 to a wealthy family in Ulm in southern Germany the young Josef Mengele studied both medicine and philosophy at university, whilst there he became particularly interested in the field of eugenics. The science of eugenics was at the peak of its popularity during the early decades of the twentieth century. Mengele's interest in eugenics was developed further when, as a young practitioner, came under the guidance of Dr. von Verschuer, a prominent German eugenicist.

During the following chapters, we shall look at how Germany's turbulent, racist and anti-Semitic society, which was particularly virulent in the post World War I Weimar Republic period, shaped the views of the young Josef Mengele. This ultimately led to him joining the Nazi party, an organization that held similar views to Mengele on the subject of eugenics. The Nazi party would also allow him free reign to conduct his ghastly experiments.

After serving with distinction on the Eastern front we shall see how the Nazis' racist and anti-Semitic policies allowed Mengele to begin his work at Auschwitz Birkenau. Here, unchecked, he was allowed to carry out numerous unethical experiments primarily on twins, young children and those that the Nazi's had deemed undesirable.

A particular favorite of Mengele's was a horrific experiment that saw him attempting to change the color of his victim's eyes. On other occasions, Mengele performed tests into how long people could endure being subjected to a series of electric shocks or experimented to see how much blood he could draw from a victim before they died. Some accounts tell how Mengele attempted to create Siamese twins with tragic consequences. As well as these ghastly experiments Josef Mengele was responsible for the deaths of many thousands of innocent people.

With the tide of the war turning and the Red Army approaching Josef Mengele, like many other war criminals, opted to run away from the scene of his crimes. After spending time in Germany, thanks in part to the occupying Allied forces presuming he was dead, Mengele decided to leave his family behind and start a new life in South America. Once in Buenos Aries, he spent time with other on the run Nazi war criminals such as Adolf Eichmann.

As the net threatened to close in on him, thanks to the work of Simon Wiesenthal amongst others, Josef Mengele moved again. First he settled in Paraguay before entering Brazil. Despite attempts by the authorities Mengele continued to remain at large. This was thanks mainly to the secrecy and diligence of those who aided him. Campaigns by Nazi hunters as well as a mock trial held in Jerusalem helped to highlight Mengele's case in the consciousness of the general public. This mock trial also served to show the world the barbarity of Josef Mengele's deeds.

It was in Brazil, whilst staying with friends, that the unrepentant Josef Mengele would die. His health had been failing for some time before he suffered a final, fatal stroke. Josef Mengele was buried under a false name and his death was to remain a secret for almost ten years. When the authorities were alerted to the possibility that Mengele had died his body was exhumed and tests were carried out. It was only then that they were sure that the man who had terrorized Auschwitz Birkenau, the Angel of Death, was finally dead.

Josef Mengele's Childhood and Early Life

Karl and Walburga Mengele lived in Gunzburg, near Ulm in southern Germany. Karl Mengele was the founder of Mengele and Son's, a company that manufactured farm machinery. On the 16th of March 1911 Walburga gave birth to her first child, the couples eldest son, Josef Mengele. Two younger brothers Karl Jr and Alois soon joined Josef to complete the family. The Mengele family was well thought of and respected in the area. They were also comfortably well off and the children enjoyed a good childhood.

The young Josef Mengele was a more than able pupil and did well in school. Not solely academic Mengele was also interested in music, art and skiing. This was in spite of being diagnosed as having osteomyelitis. After leaving school Mengele considered becoming a dentist however after discussing matters with his friend Julius Diesbach he decided on a career in medicine with a particular emphasis on "anthropology and human genetics". In April 1930 Josef Mengele applied to and was accepted into Munich University where he studied philosophy and medicine. While in Munich Mengele was greatly influenced by Dr. Ernst Rudin, a leading proponent of the theory that doctors should destroy life devoid of value.

Despite being an able pupil and the product of a wealthy family the Germany within which the young Josef Mengele grew up was a turbulent one. Following the county's defeat in World War I the German economy had struggled to recover after a series of harsh reparations were inflicted upon the country under the terms of the Treaty of Versailles. The country's newly established democratic government, the Weimar Republic, struggled to wield its authority as the economy fluctuated wildly. This was not helped by events outside Germany such as the depression and the Wall Street Crash.

It was into this unsteady society that more extreme groups, such as communists and fascists, began to have their voices heard. While anti-Semitism and racism had existed in society prior to World War I it now became more visible and distinctly nastier in tone, with many blaming the Jewish people for the failings of the state. Many of the more extreme groups sought to fuel this feeling of resentment and often preached hate against the Jews and other minority racial groups. There was also a great deal of resentment felt towards the victorious Allies for inflicting such harsh terms on the Germany following World War I. This resentment was common amongst many of the German people and the more extreme groups sought to exploit that feeling.

It was in this turbulent climate that, whilst studying in Munich, the young Josef Mengele first came into contact with the Nazi party. Like many young men the movement and its charismatic leader intrigued Mengele. In 1931, Josef Mengele joined the youth wing of the Stahlhelm, Bund der Frontsoldaten. This was a paramilitary organization that was absorbed into the Nazi Sturmabteilung (Storm Detachment) in 1934.

The National Socialist German Workers' Party or the Nazi Party as it is better known was a far right political party founded in 1919 as the German Workers Party. Emerging from the German nationalist, racist and populist Freikorps paramilitary culture which fought against the communist uprisings in post World War I Germany the party was initially anti capitalist and anti bourgeois in rhetoric. By the 1930s the party's focus had shifted to a distinctly more anti Semitic and anti Marxist tone.

At this time all over the world, the science of eugenics was gaining in popularity. It was also a field in which both the Nazi party and the young Josef Mengele took a particular interest. The eugenics movement was rooted in the biological determinist ideas of Sir Francis Galton and had initially originated in the 1880s. Galton had studied the British upper classes and concluded that their social positions were due to a superior genetic make-up. The early proponents of Galton's ideas believed that the human species should take charge of its own evolution through selective breeding.

Amongst eugenicists it was commonly held belief that the Nordic, Germanic and Anglo-Saxon peoples were superior to other races. Eugenic proponents supported strict immigration and anti-miscegenation laws as well as campaigning for the forcible sterilisation of the poor, disabled and those that they perceived to be immoral. An off shoot of this school of thought was developed by African American intellectuals such as W. E. B. Du Bois and Thomas Wyatt Turner who, along with others, believed that the best blacks were as good as the best whites. Some believed that the "talented tenth" of the races should mix. W. E. B. Du Bois also believed "only fit blacks should procreate" as this would help to eradicate what he perceived to be the race's heritage of moral iniquity.

Pseudo-scientific racism, with a particularly nasty focus on eugenics, was central to many of the Nazi's beliefs. Indeed, they made much use of the trend for eugenics that had gained popularity during the early years of the twentieth century. One of the aims of the Nazi party was to unite all the German speaking people under a "people's community", what they called Volksgemeinschaft. In the course of pursuing this goal they identified groups that were "racially desirable" and sought to exclude those deemed either to be political dissidents, physically or intellectually inferior, or of a foreign race. The Nazis also sought to improve the stock of the Germanic people through racial purity and eugenics, broad social welfare programs as well as a collective subordination of individual rights, which were sacrificed for the good of the state and the "Aryan master race".

To maintain the supposed purity and strength of the Aryan race, the Nazis sought to first remove and later exterminate Jewish, Romani and Poles as well as the majority of Slavs and other supposedly undesirable races. They also targeted the physically and mentally handicapped and imposed segregation policies on homosexuals, Africans, Jehovah's Witnesses and political opponents. These policies of segregation would reach their horrific climax in what is now known as the Holocaust.

Despite voicing such unpalatable policies the Nazi party began to steadily grow in popularity. Much of the traction the party gained was a direct result of the appeal of their leader, the dangerously enigmatic Adolf Hitler.

The party's leader since 1921, Adolf Hitler was responsible from transforming the party from a disorganized rabble of thugs into a serious political party. On the 30th of January 1933 Adolf Hitler was appointed Chancellor of Germany by the ageing president Paul von Hindenburg. Upon Hindenburg's death and by manipulating the laws of state to his advantage Hitler wasted little time in establishing a totalitarian regime with himself at the head. This became known as the Third Reich. As the 1930's progressed the unsettling policies of Hitler and his party became more obvious but, despite some opposition (which was often swiftly dealt with), they were allowed to continue to their monstrous end.

As we have briefly discussed, the science of eugenics was central to the Nazi belief system. They implemented numerous racially based social policies that placed the biological improvement of the Aryan race or Germanic "Ubermenschen" (master race) at the core of everyday life. Their twisted view of eugenics was key to this.

Before the Nazi's entered power German eugenic research had followed a similar path to that in the United States and other countries. In fact, it was directly inspired by the work done by scientists in the United States, particularly in California. Now, with the encouragement of Adolf Hitler, the prominence of eugenics rose in German society. Wealthy Nazi supporters, and those wishing to gain favor with the new political force, began to invest heavily in the science; particularly the aspects that were best suited and easily shaped to support the Nazi's racial policies.

Initially those humans targeted for destruction under the Nazi eugenics policies were living in private and state-operated institutions. They were isolated from society, and often viewed by their families as an embarrassment or an inconvenience- societies view of disability at the time was not as enlightened as it is today. As a result, these people were an easy target. When the state began to identify them as "unworthy of life" much of the rest of society either didn't notice or didn't care.

This first group to be targeted by the Nazis policy included prisoners, degenerates and dissidents as well as people suffering from congenital cognitive and physical disabilities. This final term encompassed a wide range of illnesses, from those deemed to be "feeble-minded", the epileptic, schizophrenic or manic-depressive as well as those suffering from cerebral palsy, muscular dystrophy, deafness and blindness. Homosexuals, the insane and weak were also targeted. Ultimately more than 400,000 people were sterilized against their will while over 70,000 people were killed under Action T4, which was an early Nazi euthanasia program.

As the Nazi party slowly began to implement this policy of ethnic and social cleansing in 1935 Josef Mengele gained a PhD in physical anthropology from the University of Munich. Mengele then moved to Leipzig where he was employed at the Leipzig University Clinic. In January 1937 Mengele became a research assistant studying physical anthropology, genetics and twins at the Institute for

Hereditary Biology and Racial Hygiene in Frankfurt. Here he was to fall under the guidance of Doctor Otmar Freiherr von Verschuer.

Doctor von Verschuer was regarded as a pioneer in the twin methodology in genetics research and in the study of the inheritance of diseases and anomalies. This work had le to von Verschuer becoming a prominent eugenicist within German scientific circles. A man who held a particularly strong interest in racial hygiene it is therefore unsurprising to learn that Von Verschuer was also an advocate of compulsory sterilisation, a policy that was also popular with the Nazi party.

In Frankfurt Mengele aided von Verschuer in conducting genetic research. Their work focused primarily on twins. Josef Mengele also conducted research into genetic factors that result in deformities like cleft lip and palate or cleft chin. In 1938 Mengele published a thesis on the subject that earned him a cum laude doctorate in medicine. It has been argued that despite what he would later do the works that Mengele published during this period deviates little from the scientific mainstream of the time. Irrespective of who published them they would have been viewed as valid scientific efforts in many of the world's countries at this time.

Away from his work Josef Mengele married Irene Schönbein in 1939. The pair had enjoyed a long courtship after meeting while Josef Mengele was beginning his medical career working as a medical resident in Leipzig. However, because of Mengele's work in the Nazi party during World War II the couple did not spend much time together. On her infrequent visits to see Josef, Irene recorded in her diary how much she disliked the atmosphere and the smell of the camps where her husband spent much of his time.

Despite this almost constant separation the Mengele's did have a child. Their son child, Rolf was born in 1944. Rolf would not meet his father until he was 16 years old because while Rolf was growing up Josef Mengele was either working in the Nazi death camps or on the run as wanted war criminal, hiding in South America.

Back in 1939 and Hitler's constant quest for Lebensraum had pushed the other European powers to the brink of war. When Germany invaded Poland in September 1939 Great Britain and the Allied powers declared war on Nazi Germany.

Mengele's Role in World War II

Despite their mutual interest in eugenics and his earlier membership of the Stahlhelm, Bund der Frontsoldaten Josef Mengele had not yet formally joined the Nazi party. This he corrected in 1937. This lapse may suggest someone who was not committed to the Nazi cause but instead someone looking to use membership of the party to further their career or social standing. Josef Mengele's actions over the course of the next few years would reveal his true colors as a committed believer in the Nazi cause of an Aryan society.

As we have discussed in the previous chapter the ideology of Nazism brought together elements of anti-Semitism, racial hygiene and eugenics, combining them with the desire to unite all the German-speaking people into one state. Many of these ideals, particularly the scientific elements not only appealed to Mengele but tied in closely to his own scientific interests.

Once a member of the Nazi party Josef Mengele then applied to join the Schutzstaffel, better known as the SS. He was accepted in May 1938, around the same time Mengele enrolled in the Institute of Biological Inheritance and Race Hygiene in Frankfurt. Two months later Mengele was awarded his medical degree by the University of Frankfurt and subsequently published his medical dissertation. During this period Josef Mengele would publish a number of papers and studies such as "Genealogical Studies in the Cases of Cleft Lip, Jaw and Palate" or, from his time working in Munich

"Racial Morphological Examination of the Anterior Portion of the Lower Jaw in Four Racial Groups".

When not working Josef Mengele was like many of the new SS recruits, receiving basic training. The Gebirgsjager or mountain infantry carried out the majority of this training. As well as basic combat instructions the training regime also saw Mengele spend time skiing in the Snalfedon Tyrol. Despite being a qualified medic the SS expected Mengele and all the other medics in their ranks to be able to fight and kill should the circumstances demand it. Away from his military training Josef Mengele continued his medical work.

Following the outbreak of World War II Mengele initially continued to work at the Frankfurt Institute alongside von Verschuer. He also spent a short time at the University Clinic in Bonn and, in his spare time, attended SS indoctrination classes. Josef Mengele also found time to publish a research paper concerning the inheritance of ear fistules. Upon receiving his call up to the Werhmacht Mengele requested to join the medical service of the Waffen-SS.

In August 1940 Josef Mengele was made a SS Untersturmfuhrer (second lieutenant). Mengele was then posted to Nazi occupied territories in Poland where he was attached to the Genealogical Section of the Race & Resettlement Office. During this period Josef Mengele was to prove himself to be a keen and able member of the SS Mengele, he also gained the attention of his superiors.

The fighting on the Eastern front had arisen because of a desire by both the Nazis and the

Soviet Union to claim the lands of Eastern Europe for their own gains. Despite their ideological antipathy Nazi Germany and the Soviet Union were both unsatisfied with the outcome of World War I. Russia had lost substantial territories in Eastern Europe thanks to the Treaty of Brest-Litovsk (1918). This treaty ceded control of Poland, Lithuania, Estonia, Latvia, Finland, and other areas, to the Central Powers. The turmoil caused by the subsequent Russian Revolution meant that when the territories were liberated under the terms of the Paris Peace Conference of 1919 Soviet Russia was not represented. They did not therefore regain their lost lands.

The Molotov- Ribbentrop Pact, (1939) was a non-aggression agreement signed between Nazi Germany and the Soviet Union. It contained a secret protocol aiming to return

Central Europe to the state it was in before World War I. This would see Finland, Estonia, Latvia and Lithuania would return to Russian (Soviet) control, while Poland and Romania would be divided between the two powers.

In September 1939 the Soviet Union and Nazi Germany invaded Poland and partitioned it. After Finland refused the terms of a Soviet pact of mutual assistance, the Soviet Union attacked Finland on 30 November 1939 in what became known as the Winter War. This was a bitter and hard fought conflict that resulted in a peace treaty, which was signed on the 13th of March 1940 and saw Finland maintain its independence despite losing some land in Karelia. Meanwhile the Soviet Union was busy reclaiming much of its lost Baltic territories safe in the knowledge that the Molotov–Ribbentrop Pact ostensibly provided security to them in the occupation both of the Baltics and of the north and northeastern regions of Romania.

However, Adolf Hitler was keen to secure Lebensraum (living space) for the peoples of his German Reich. He identified the lands of Eastern Europe and in particular Russia as an ideal place for his "master race" to settle. There was also a desire to capture the Russian oil fields to help power the Reich. Nazi rhetoric had for years painted the Soviets as a sub human enemy. Operation Barbarossa, the name given to the German invasion of the Soviet Union, was therefore a popular move amongst the majority of the German people.

Launched in June 1941 the German invasion of the Soviet Union was initially successful. The German's Blitzkrieg tactics saw them quickly push the Soviet Union forces back through the

Ukraine. As the Red Army withdrew behind the Dnieper and Dvina rivers, the Soviet Stavka (high command) turned its attention to evacuating as much of the western regions' industry as it could. Factories were dismantled and transported on flatcars away from the front line for re-establishment in more remote areas of the Ural Mountains, Caucasus, Central Asia and southeastern Siberia. The focus on the evacuation of industry meant that the civilian population was left to make their own way east, if they were unable to evacuate they were left behind to the mercy of the invading forces.

This scorched earth policy that the Red Army implemented was intended to deny the invading Nazi forces easy access to basic supplies. Stalin went so far as to form special destruction battalions in the front line areas with the specific orders to execute any suspicious person as well as burning down villages, schools, and public buildings. As a part of this policy, the thousands of anti-Soviet prisoners were also massacred.

Despite the invasion's early success, and ignoring the fact that winter was approaching, Hitler was keen for his forces to capture Moscow. Operation Typhoon, which began on the 30th of September, saw the 2nd Panzer Army rush along the paved road from Oryol to the Oka River at Plavsk, while the 4th Panzer Army and 3rd Panzer armies surrounded the Soviet forces in two huge pockets at Vyazma and Bryansk. Army Group North positioned itself in front of Leningrad and attempted to cut the rail link at Mga to the east. This began the 900-day Siege of Leningrad.

The intense fighting continued throughout the autumn. The onset of the winter freeze saw one last German lunge that began on the 15th of November, when the Wehrmacht attempted to encircle Moscow. On the 27th of November, the 4th Panzer Army got to within 19 miles of the Kremlin when it reached the last tram stop of the Moscow line at Khimki. However, by the 6th of December it had become clear that the Wehrmacht did not have the strength to capture Moscow, and the attack was suspended.

The Soviet troops, under the leadership of Marshal Shaposhnikov, thus began his counter-attack. Employing freshly mobilized and well supplied reserves, as well as some well-trained Far-Eastern divisions transferred from the east following intelligence that Japan would remain neutral they attacked the tiring German forces.

By now the German army was struggling to get supplies and reinforcements to their front line troops. Their efforts were not helped by the harsh Russian winter. The Soviet counter attack during the Battle of Moscow had removed the immediate German threat to the city and the fighting which now followed was some of the most intense and horrific of the entire war. It was, many believe, also the turning point of World War II. As the eastern front took up more and more resources the Allies began to make gains on the western front. As a result, the now depleted and under supplied Wehrmacht had ceased to look invincible. The momentum had swung to the Soviet Union and Allied forces.

In June 1941 when Mengele was transferred to the Ukraine much of this was still to come. Whilst serving here his efforts saw him be awarded the Iron Cross, Second Class. January 1942 brought yet another change as Josef Mengele was sent to join the 5th SS Panzer Division Wiking where he served as a battalion medical office. During one particularly heavy engagement with the forces of the Soviet Union, Josef Mengele rescued two German soldiers from a burning tank. These heroic actions led to him being awarded the Iron Cross, First Class as well as the Black Wound Badge and the Medal for the Care of the German People.

Later that year, during fighting near Rostov-on-Don Josef Mengele was seriously wounded. Despite making a full recovery he was now deemed unfit for active, front line service despite this being a period in which the German forces were starting to become severely depleted. Instead of being discharged from the SS Josef Mengele was transferred to the Rasse und Siedlungshauptamt (Race and Resettlement Office) in Berlin. It was here, the Nazi authorities deemed, that his particular talents and interests could best be put to use.

This posting also allowed Mengele to resume his association with von Verschuer who was still working at the Kaiser Wilhelm Institute of Anthropology, Human Heredity and Eugenics. By the end of the year Josef Mengele had been made the medical expert for the Race and Resettlement Main Office. In 1943 Mengele was promoted to the rank of SS Hauptsturmfuhrer (Captain).

In early 1943 von Verschuer encouraged Mengele to apply to be transferred to a place where he could undertake genetic research on human subjects. Seeing the opportunity Josef Mengele duly applied and was subsequently accepted. On the 30th of May 1943 Chief Medical Officer SS-Standortarzt Eduard Wirths appointed Mengele chief physician of the Ziegunerfamilienlager (Romani family camp). He was to be based in the sub camp of Birkenau at Auschwitz concentration camp.

It was here at Auschwitz Birkenau that Mengele would do the work that would render him infamous in the annuls of history. As well as personally sending thousands to the gas chambers Mengele performed countless unethical experiments on children, twins and other people who interested him. Those who did not die as a result of his work were often killed after they had ceased to be useful. Those who survived were often maimed for life. Mengele also performed experiments on people trying to change their eye colour as well as infecting people with diseases. Many prisoners who were qualified medical practitioners were forced to help Mengele carry out his inhuman work.

Auschwitz Birkenau

Today the Holocaust is viewed as one of humanities darkest periods. The architects of it are viewed as some of history's biggest monsters. It is thought that some six million European Jews lost their lives in these camps. This total equates to almost two thirds of the nine million Jews who were known to be living in Continental Europe at the time. It is believed that 1.5 million of the Jewish lives lost were children. As well as the Jewish population the Nazis and their collaborators also targeted the Roma, ethnic Poles, various Slavic ethnic groups, Soviet citizens, prisoners of war, homosexuals, Jehovah Witnesses, black people, the physically and mentally disabled, political opponents and dissidents and those who they deemed to be "incurably sick".

In the years from 1941 to the end of World War II in 1945 the Nazis and their collaborators systematically arranged for the murder of large groups of people who they deemed undesirable. Largely coordinated by the SS, but under direction from the highest parts of the Nazi leadership, every arm of the German bureaucratic system was involved in the logistics of organized mass murder. These killings occurred throughout the German occupied territories. Over 42,000 camps, ghettos and other detention sites were established specifically for this purpose. It is the systematic, bureaucratic nature of the Holocaust that makes it all the more disturbing.

The deadly persecution was not immediate but rather was implemented in stages. This culminated in the Final Solution, the name given to the policy of mass extermination. Since

Hitler's rise to power in 1933 the Nazi government had passed a series of laws designed to exclude the Jewish population from civil society, such as places of education and employment. The most prominent of these laws was the 1935 Nuremberg Laws, which deprived Jews of the right to hold German citizenship.

From 1933 onwards the Nazis built a network of concentration camps throughout Germany. These were to hold political opponents and those deemed "undesirable". Following the German invasion of Poland in 1939 the Nazi regime set up ghettos. These were designed to segregate the Jewish populace from the rest of society. It also made it easier for them to be removed from what was termed the Greater German Reich.

In 1941, as German forces captured huge territories in the East, all anti-Jewish measures were radicalized. Specialized paramilitary units called Einsatzgruppen were formed. These groups were ordered to murder around two million Jews in mass shootings. This they achieved in less than a year. By mid-1942, victims were being deported from the ghettos in sealed freight trains to extermination camps fitted with gas chambers. Thousands did not survive the journey.

Jewish resistance, although severely limited in terms of resources, was offered in over 100 locations, most notably during the Warsaw Ghetto uprising of 1943, when thousands of Jewish fighters held the Waffen-SS at bay for four weeks. Millions of Jews, Soviet POWs, Roma, and others died in the concentration camps. The killing continued until the end of World War II in Europe in late April 1945.

Often thought of as just one camp Auschwitz concentration camp was in fact a network of concentration and extermination camps. These were built and operated by the German Nazi regime during the Third Reich. Auschwitz was located in Poland in land annexed by the occupying German forces. As well as the original Auschwitz camp there was also Auschwitz II Birkenau, which was a concentration and extermination camp, Auschwitz III Monowitz a labor camp supplying forced labor to a nearby IG Farben factory and 45 other smaller satellite camps.

Auschwitz I had initially been constructed for the purpose of holding Polish political prisoners. The first intake arrived in May 1940.

Over a year later in September 1941 the first extermination of prisoners took place. Existing alongside the original camp Auschwitz II Birkenau would become one of the major sites for the Nazi Final Solution. The Final Solution was the name given to the mass extermination of the Jewish people.

From early 1942 until late 1944, transport trains delivered Jews to the camp's gas chambers from all over the occupied territories. Upon their arrival the SS, who had devised a ruthless selection process, greeted them. Those deemed able to work were admitted into the labor camp while those unfit for work were taken straight to the gas chambers. Here they were ruthlessly killed en masse through exposure to the deadly pesticide Zyklon B.

It is estimated that 1.3 million people were sent to the Auschwitz camp alone. At least 1.1 million of these people died here. Around 90 percent of those killed here were Jewish. It has been approximated that 1 in 6 of the Jews killed in the Holocaust died at Auschwitz. However, it was not just the Jews who suffered.

Others deported to Auschwitz included 150,000 Poles, 23,000 Romani and Sinti, 15,000 Soviet Union prisoners of war, 400 Jehovah's Witnesses and tens of thousands of others from a variety of nationalities. A large number of these other victims were homosexuals. Those not earmarked for the gas chambers died as a result of forced labor, starvation, infectious diseases individual executions, and medical experiments. It was also not just at Auschwitz where people died; the Nazis had a number of death camps of which Auschwitz is, today, one of the most well-known.

Over the course of its existence the camp was staffed by 7,000 members of the German SS. Approximately 12 percent of these were later convicted of war crimes. Some of these, including camp commandant Rudolf Höss, were executed for their role in the atrocities. The initial reports of the horrors of Auschwitz had seemed unbelievable, so much so that the Allied powers had, at first, refused to believe them. This disbelief is the reason behind the Allies failure not to bomb the camps upon first learning of their existence. This decision remains controversial to this day.

Due to the location of the camp and the condition in which the prisoners were kept successful escapes were rare. One hundred forty-four prisoners are known to have escaped from Auschwitz successfully. On the 7th of October 1944, two Sonderkommando units — prisoners assigned to staff the gas chambers — launched a brief, unsuccessful uprising.

As the liberating Soviet Union troops worked their way towards Auschwitz in January 1945 the SS forced the inhabitants on what has been described as a death march to the west. Those prisoners who were left behind at the camp were liberated on the 27th of January 1945. This is now commemorated as International Holocaust Remembrance Day. In the decades following the camps liberation its prominence in the popular culture grew as the survivors wrote memoirs and shared their experiences. These include Primo Levi, Viktor Frankl, and Elie Wiesel. The remains of the camp were to become a dominant symbol of the Holocaust and in 1947 Poland founded the Auschwitz-Birkenau State Museum on the site of Auschwitz I and II.

Despite attempts by the SS and Nazis to hide the horrors of the Holocaust, they burnt records and killed many of the prisoners as the liberating Allied forces approached today the holocaust is remembered and condemned by the vast majority of people as a horrific and depraved act which can never be allowed to happen again. Despite this, to this day, mass genocides continue to happen in places all over the world. While these are all horrific none have yet come close to the systematic, organized mass murder implemented by the Nazi party and their collaborators in Europe in the late 1930s and 1940s.

In 1943 the true horrors of the Holocaust were only just beginning. If those deemed undesirable by the Nazis survived the trip to Auschwitz, many didn't, as they were already weak and unwell after years of persecution and victimization at the hands of the Nazis; they were met by the SS who had devised a ruthlessly efficient selection process. Those deemed fit to work were sent to the labor camp while those selected to die were sent to the gas chambers. The majority of those selected to die were children, pregnant women or those women caring for small children, the elderly and those who appeared, after a cursory inspection, to be unfit for work. While both of these fates were horrible there was a third group to which nobody would want to belong.

Many of those who arrived on these cattle trains would have seen a slightly built man keenly observing the new arrivals. Neatly dressed in a dark green tunic with barely a hair out of place. His SS cap tilted to one side while his hand rested on his pistol belt. A flick of his cane, which was clasped in a gloved hand, was enough to separate families, singling out those who interested him. The prisoners knew this man as the Angel of Death. To his friends and colleagues, he was Doctor Josef Mengele.

As part of his work at the camps Mengele was, like all the other camp doctors, required to participate in this selection process of new arrivals. Often Josef Mengele turned up to the selection process even when he was not assigned to do so in the hope of finding suitable subjects for his experiments. He was particularly interested in finding sets of twins. It has been reported that in contrast to most of the doctors who undertook this task and viewed it as one of their most stressful and horrible duties Josef Mengele undertook the task with a smile on his face, often whistling a jaunty tune.

Initially one of the reasons for Josef Mengele being sent to Auschwitz Birkenau was to investigate the causes of, and find a way of immunizing against, malaria. It has been recorded that Mengele himself contracted malaria whilst based at Auschwitz but was able to recover from the disease. This was not the only time that Mengele's work threatened his health. On another occasion Mengele was recommended by Dr. Wirths for the War Service Cross for "combating a severe typhoid infection though he was infected himself with a very heavy typhus".

Despite his position of chief physician of the Ziegunerfamilienlager Josef Mengele, like the other SS doctors, did not treat the camp inmates. Instead they supervised the activities of the inmate doctors who worked in the camp medical service. Mengele, like the other SS Doctors, would make weekly visits to the hospital barracks. Those who had not recovered after two weeks of treatment were sent to the gas chambers.

Instead of helping the sick Mengele was one of a team of doctors responsible for administrating Zyklon B, this is a cyanide based pesticide and was used in the gas chambers at Birkenau. Josef Mengele was responsible for administering the gas into chambers located in crematoria IV and V.

In 1943 an outbreak of noma, a gangrenous bacterial disease of the mouth and face, struck the Romani camp. Mengele saw the opportunity to initiate a study to determine the cause of the disease and to possibly develop a treatment. With the aid of a Jewish pediatrician Dr. Berthold Epstein, who prior to his detention in Auschwitz Birkenau had been a professor at Prague University, Mengele was able to isolate those suffering from the disease in a separate barrack. Mengele also had several of the afflicted children killed and their heads and organs preserved. These were then sent to the SS Medical Academy in Graz as well as other facilities in order for them to be studied. This study continued until the camp was liquidated in 1944.

When a typhus epidemic broke out in the women's camp Mengele cleared a block of 600

Jewish women and sent them to the gas chamber. With those infected now dead Mengele had the empty block cleaned and disinfected while the occupants of a neighboring block were bathed, de-loused and given new clothing. They were then moved into the clean block. This process was repeated until all the barracks were disinfected. A similar process would occur when other diseases, such as scarlet fever, broke out at the camp. For his efforts, Mengele was promoted in 1944 to First Physician of the Auschwitz Birkenau sub camp.

Infamously Mengele also used his time at Auschwitz to continue his anthropological studies and research on hereditary genetics. He was freely allowed to use the camp's inmates as human guinea pigs. These experiments were conducted with little or no regard for the health, safety, physical or emotional well-being of the victim. As we have previously seen at the selection process Mengele was particularly interested in identical twins.

As he surveyed the new arrivals at the camp Mengele occasionally came alive. Often when he spotted a set of twins. He particularly liked identical twins.

Josef Mengele was reportedly fanatical about drawing blood from twins. It is said that Mengele often bled people to death in this manner. He would also pick out people with eyes of two different colors, heterochromia iridum, dwarfs and other physical abnormalities. According to those who worked alongside him Josef Mengele liked to carry out electric shock endurance tests on female inmates in the camp.

Applied for by von Verschuer, a grant was provided to Mengele by the Deutsche Forschungsgemeinschaft. In return Mengele regularly sent von Verschuer reports and shipments of specimens from his work at the camp. The money provided by this grant was used to build a pathology laboratory attached to Crematorium II at Birkenau. Dr. Miklós Nyiszli, a Hungarian Jewish pathologist who had arrived at the camp on the 29th of May 1944, performed dissections and prepared specimens for shipment in this laboratory. He did so under the direction of Josef Mengele.

Josef Mengele's twin research was partly intended to prove the supremacy of hereditary genetics over the environment in which you live, or put simply to prove that nature trumped nurture. In doing so he intended to scientifically enforce the Nazi belief in the superiority of the Aryan race. Dr Miklós Nyiszli, as well as others who were put to work in Auschwitz Birkenau alongside Mengele, later suggested that Mengele's particular interest in twins may have also been motivated by a desire to improve the reproduction rate of the German race by bettering the chances of racially desirable people having twins.

Those selected by Mengele for his experiments were better fed and housed than the other camp inmates. They were also temporarily safe meeting their end in the gas chambers. Mengele also established a kindergarten for the children of his subjects and all the Romani children who were six years old or younger. Like the conditions his subjects lived in this facility provided better food and living conditions than other areas of the camp. It even had a playground. On his regular visits to the children's facility "Uncle Mengele" as he insisted the children call him, would distribute sweets and other goodies.

This veneer of geniality frequently slipped. "Uncle" Mengele was also personally responsible for the deaths of many of these children either via lethal injection, shootings, and beatings or as a consequence of his experiments. Many of the twins who came under the attention of Mengele and survived later recalled him as a gentle, affable man who befriended them, passing them sweets and chocolates. As many, on arrival at the camp, had been separated from their family they saw Mengele as a father figure of sorts. Despite this they were aware that they could be killed at any time if they were singled out. The older children were fully aware of Mengele's split personality and tried to encourage the younger children to keep a low profile to avoid his deathly attention.

The twins whom Mengele acquired were subject to weekly examinations. These included measurements of their physical attributes. He would also frequently perform unnecessary experiments and operations such as the amputation of limbs or the deliberate injection of one twin with typhus or some other horrible disease and the transfusion of blood from one twin into the other. Many victims died as a result of, or during, these experiments. If one twin died from the disease Mengele would have the other twin killed so that he could perform comparative post- mortems.

Once the experiments were concluded the twins, if they had survived, were often now deemed to have outlived their usefulness. It was normal practice for the twins to now be killed before their bodies were dissected. Dr. Nyiszli described that on one occasion Mengele personally killed fourteen twins in one night by giving them a chloroform injection to the heart. Mengele then began dissecting and meticulously noting each and every piece of the twins' bodies.

There are numerous, tragic stories of people who encountered Josef Mengele in Auschwitz Birkenau. One such story is that of Eva Mozes and her identical twin, Miriam. Despite coming to Mengele's attention the twins were fortunate in that they managed to survive Mengele's deadly genetic experiments at the camp. However, after their liberation the Mozes girls learnt that their parents, grandparents, two older sisters, uncles, aunts and cousins had all been killed in the Holocaust. After the liberation of the camp, Eva and Miriam were the first two twins in the famous footage filmed by the Soviets, which is often shown in footage about the horrors of Holocaust.

Mengele's fascination with eye color, particularly people with different colored eyes, led to some of his more horrific experiments. Mengele attempted to change people's eye color by injecting chemicals into the eyes of living subjects. He also killed people with heterochromatic eyes so that the eyes could be removed and sent to Berlin for detailed study.

When it came to dwarfs and people with physical abnormalities Mengele was just as unrestrained in his investigations. He would take physical measurements, draw blood, extract healthy teeth, and subject people to the injection of unnecessary drugs and X-rays.

Again after the subjects had been investigated, a period of around two weeks usually, if they were still alive many of the victims were sent to the gas chambers. Their skeletons were then sent to Berlin for further study.

Mengele also sought out pregnant women, on whom he would perform experiments before sending them to the gas chambers. One witness, Vera Alexander, described how on one occasion Mengele sewed two Romani twins together back to back in an attempt to create conjoined twins. After days of suffering the poor children died of gangrene.

The strict veil of secrecy, which surrounded the experiments and events at Auschwitz Birkenau, allowed Mengele to carry out these unethical experiments largely unhindered and also to work with gruesome efficiency. The full extent of his work, and the true number of people who suffered at his hands will probably never be known. The records that Mengele meticulously sent to Dr. Von Verschuer at the Kaiser Wilhelm Institute were, when the tide of the war turned, shipped out in two truckloads and destroyed in an attempt to hide what had been allowed to happen. The notes and records that Mengele kept with him, and probably took to South America have never been found.

Mengele was not the only SS doctor who was acting in this manner. Also based at Auschwitz Dr. Herta Oberhauser is known to have killed children with oil and evipan injections, removed their limbs and vital organs, rubbed ground glass and sawdust into wounds. After the war she was convicted of war crimes and sentenced to twenty years imprisonment. Released early, in 1952, she became a family doctor at Stocksee in Germany before her license to practice medicine was revoked in 1960. Others who worked at the camps and were deemed to have been responsible for the treatment of their prisoners were, once convicted, sentenced to death.

After World War II Mengele Goes to South America

As the Allied forces began to close in, at the death camps an order to cut expenses and save on gas usage led to an order to place living children directly into the ovens or throw them into open burning pits. Many of those who worked at the camps realized that the net was closing in around them. Realizing that time was running out Josef Mengele made arrangements to leave Auschwitz disguised as a member of the regular German infantry.

As the troops of the Soviet Union approached Auschwitz Josef Mengele, like many others, fled. Mengele left Auschwitz Birkenau for the final time on the 17th of January 1945. It is believed that from there Mengele made his way to the Gross-Rosen Concentration camp in Lower Silesia. He brought with him two boxes of specimens and records of his experiments. Most of the Auschwitz camp medical records had already been destroyed by the SS. Ten days later on the 27th of January the Red Army liberated Auschwitz.

Just before the Gross-Rosen camp was liberated on the 11th of February 1945 Mengele again fled. This time he made his way west. Josef Mengele was now disguising himself as a Wehrmacht officer. In Saaz (now Zatec) he entrusted his incriminating Auschwitz documents to a nurse with whom he had struck up a relationship. Now free from these incriminating papers Mengele carried on further into Germany. After spending some time in Matthausen he moved again. This time Josef Mengele was not so lucky.

As he attempted to travel near Munich Josef Mengele was arrested and detained as a prisoner of war by the liberating American army. However, in a twist of fate and despite being held under his real name Josef Mengele wasn't permanently detained. The authorities had failed to recognize the man they held prisoner.

This failure was later put down to the disorganization of the Allies with regards to distributing accurate wanted lists. It also helped Mengele that he did not have the customary SS blood group tattoo like many of his contemporaries. As a result, nobody identified Josef Mengele as being a suspect on the major war criminal list.

Despite his wanted status Mengele worked as a farmhand for Georg and Maria Fischer in Rosenheim, Bavaria in Germany from the summer of 1945 up until the spring of 1949. For this work he earned 10 marks a week. While this was a bold move Mengele was astute enough to obtain a false identity, easy enough to do in the chaotic climate of immediate post war Germany. During this period Mengele lived under the name of Fritz Ullman, he later altered the surname to Hollmann. He also managed to journey to the Soviet occupied area of Germany to recover his Auschwitz records.

What helped Mengele in his ability to remain a free man was the fact that the authorities and initially his family believed that he had died in the fighting as the Russian army advanced towards Berlin. Despite telling the investigating Allied authorities this, when Irene learnt that

Josef Mengele was still alive she maintained the charade that her husband had died. The couple met on a couple of occasions in this chaotic post war period before Josef Mengele decided to leave for a new life in South America. As his wife refused to accompany him on the journey the couple now formally separated, a few years later Josef Mengele and his first wife Irene formally divorced.

With the help of his prosperous family and a network of former SS members Josef Mengele carefully managed to arrange for his safe passage to South America. On the 17th of April 1948 Mengele arrived at an inn at Steinbach. Here he spent the night just 400 yards from the Italian border. The next day Mengele was guided through the Brenner Pass and then headed towards Vipiteno where he was put up at the Golden Cross Inn.

Mengele stayed in the area for a month, until he was able to acquire a new identity and an International Red Cross passport. Despite being arrested in May 1948 for trying to bribe an official in an attempt to obtain an Italian exit visa and spending three weeks in jail Josef Mengele still remained undetected. In July 1949 under an assumed identity Doctor Josef Mengele boarded the 'North King' bound for Buenos Aires, Argentina.

After settling in Buenos Aires Mengele first found work as a carpenter. During this period, he is known to have resided in a boarding house in the Vicente Lopez suburb. From there Mengele then moved to the house of a known Nazi sympathizer in the affluent Florida neighborhood of Buenos Aires. Now settled Josef Mengele started to work as a salesman for his family's farm equipment company. From

1951 on, and whilst acting in the role of regional sales representative, Mengele was able to make frequent and regular trips to Paraguay.

Whilst in Buenos Aires in 1952, Josef Mengele spent time in the company of Adolf Eichmann and Hans Ulrich Rudel. Like Mengele these men were also Nazi war criminals on the run and living under assumed identities. By 1953 Josef Mengele was living in an apartment in the center of Buenos Airies. The following year Mengele rented a house in the Buenos Aries suburb of Olivos. It is clear the Josef Mengele was comfortable in this new country and was beginning to do well in his new life.

In 1956 Mengele obtained a copy of his birth certificate through the West German embassy and was subsequently issued with an Argentine foreign residence permit under his real name.

This document allowed him to obtain a West German passport, also under his real name. Encouraged by this Mengele embarked on a visit to Europe. Here he met up in Switzerland for a ski holiday with his son Rolf who was told that Mengele was his "Uncle Fritz". Josef Mengele also met his widowed sister-in-law Martha, and spent a week in his hometown of Günzburg. It seems that Martha and Josef Mengele grew close during this brief visit.

Emboldened by his successful journey upon his return to Argentina in September, Mengele began to live under his real name. About a month after he returned to South America Martha, his sister in law, and her son Karl Heinz, Mengele's nephew, followed him. The three took up residence together. Josef Mengele married his second wife Martha while they were on holiday in Uruguay in 1958. Upon their return to Argentina the couple bought a house in Buenos Aires.

Mengele was now doing quite well in his new life. His business interests now included part ownership of Fadro Farm, a pharmaceutical company and it seems that he also continued to practice medicine. In 1958 a teenage girl died following an illegal abortion. This prompted the authorities to arrest several doctors as well as Josef Mengele. Josef Mengele was questioned under suspicion of practicing medicine without a license. He was subsequently released without charge. This story was confirmed in 1992 when the Argentine government released files that seemed to confirm that Mengele had indeed practiced medicine without a license and was known to carry out illegal abortions.

Despite being released Mengele now became concerned that the publicity from his run in with the law would lead to his Nazi background and wartime activities being discovered. Hoping to once again successfully disappear Mengele took an extended business trip to Paraguay. By this time, he knew the country well. During this extended visit Josef Mengele managed to obtain Paraguayan citizenship under the name José Mengele.

Mengele now sought to build a new life for himself in yet another new country. Despite settling here in 1959 it is known that after this Josef Mengele returned to Buenos Aires several times in order to wrap up his business affairs and visit his family. His second wife and stepson remained in Buenos Aries until December 1960. During this period Martha and

Karl Heinz lived in a boarding house in the city. They subsequently returned home to Germany.

It is a curious point of interest that Josef Mengele the notorious war criminal was able to live so openly during this period. This is in spite of Mengele's name being mentioned several times during the Nuremberg trials. (The Nuremberg trials saw the majority of the surviving Nazis leadership tried and sentenced for their part in World War II and the humanitarian crimes carried out by the regime.) It seems that no concerted effort was ever made by the authorities to locate Josef Mengele as the triumphant Allied forces were convinced that he was dead. Irene and Mengele's family in Günzburg certainly told the authorities that they believed this to be the case, despite knowing that he was in South America.

Despite the presumed demise of Josef Mengele whilst working in West Germany, Nazi hunters Simon Wiesenthal and Hermann Langbein proceeded to collect information from witnesses detailing Mengele's wartime activities.

Simon Wiesenthal was born on the 31st of December 1908 in Buczacz in what was then Galacia. Today the place is called Buchach and is part of Ukraine. As Galacia was, at the time of Wiesenthal's birth part of the Austria- Hungary Empire, during World War I his father fought, and died, as part of the Austrian army. The Wiesenthal family also faced persecution from occupying soldiers who often singled out Jewish families. After gaining a degree in architectural engineering during the 1930s Wiesenthal set up a practice in the (now Ukranian) city of Lvov. In 1936 he married Cyla Muller.

A few years later following the Soviet occupation of the region and with Wiesenthal losing members of his stepfamily he was sent to work in a bedsprings factory. Later Wiesenthal later claimed that it was only bribery that saved him and his wife from being sent to Siberia. While this period of the young couple's life was difficult worse was to come.

Following the German occupation in 1941 Wiesenthal and his wife were placed in a forced labor camp serving the German Eastern Railway plants. Here Cyla Wiesenthal was able to pass as a Polish citizen and was transported out of the camp by an underground resistance movement. Simon Wiesenthal was interred in several different camps. On one occasion he managed to escape but was recaptured. Wiesenthal also, later admitted, that he had twice attempted suicide during this period. In

1944 Simon Wiesenthal was transported to the Janowska camp.

In 1945 Simon Wiesenthal was liberated from the Mauthausen camp in Austria by the U.S. army. Despite being severely malnourished Wiesenthal was reunited with his wife and eventually regained his health. While Simon and Cyla had survived dozens of members of their family had died alongside other victims of the Nazi Holocaust.

In response to his suffering and the loss of so many of his friends and family Simon Wiesenthal dedicated his remaining years to tracking down former Nazi's who had attempted to escape justice for what they had done during the years of the Third Reich. As well as directing the Jewish Documentation Centre in Linz and a similar organization in

Vienna he also founded the Simon Wiesenthal Centre in Los Angeles in 1977. Simon Wiesenthal was greatly acclaimed for his life's work. Wiesenthal is also credited as contributing greatly to the capture, in 1961, of Adolf Eichmann who is recognized as one of the coordinators of the Nazi's Final Solution. Wiesenthal's investigations also led to the capture of a number of other war criminals such as death camp commander Franz Stangl and Gestapo worker Karl Silberbauer who was responsible for the arrest of Anne Frank and her family.

Hermann Langbein was an Austrian who after fighting in the Spanish Civil War was interred in a series of concentration camps including Dachau and Auschwitz. He later served as General Secretary of the International Auschwitz Committee, which sought to support survivors of the camps and raise awareness of the Holocaust and anti-Semitism. Shortly after the end of World War II Langbein aided Wiesenthal in his efforts to track down escaped Nazi war criminals

In the course of this activity Langbein had cause to search through the public records. Here Langbein found Mengele's divorce papers listing an address in Buenos Aires. This alerted the authorities to the fact that the notorious Josef Mengele was still alive. It also gave them a clue as to his whereabouts. Langbein and Wiesenthal pressured West German authorities into drawing up an arrest warrant, which finally took place on the 5th of June 1959, and starting extradition proceedings. The extradition request was formally made in 1960.

Initially Argentina turned down the request on the grounds that the fugitive was no longer living at the address given on the documents. By the time extradition was approved, on the 30th of June 1960, Josef Mengele had already fled to Paraguay. Here he was living on a farm near the Argentine border. From this farm Mengele made arrangements to move once again. In October 1960 Josef Mengele entered Brazil. After his departure a friend, Wolfgang Gerhard, sold his land in Paraguay for $20,000.

In 1961 and now living under the alias of Peter Hochbichlet, Mengele was introduced to Mr. Gaza Stammer and his wife by a mutual friend, Wolfgang Gerhard. While Josef Mengele continued to live in South America Wiesenthal received information placing the wanted man in a variety of locations including, in 1960, on the Greek island of Kythnos, in 1961 in Cairo, in

Spain in 1971 and in Paraguay in 1978, eighteen years after he had left. In 1968 Erich Erdstein a former Brazilian police officer claims to have killed Josef Mengele.

In 1964 the Bonn Foreign Ministry announced, "We can confirm that Mengele is a citizen of Paraguay". This was followed by the Chief Prosecutor for Hesse raising the reward for Josef Mengele's capture from 20,000 DM to 50,000 DM. Despite this ever increasing bounty those hiding Josef Mengele remained steadfast in their determination to keep him safe.

In 1964 the Paraguayan Government announced that Josef Mengele had left Paraguay four years previously for Brazil. The following year the authorities in Bonn begin extradition proceedings in Brazil where the CIA reported, "Mengele is rumored to have gone to

Matto Grosso". With the net ever tightening around him in 1969 Josef Mengele moved to Jardin Luciana where he reportedly resides in a villa near Franco de Rocha. So well-kept was the secret of Josef Mengele's location that in 1970 the US Government publicly admitted that it didn't know where he was.

While Nazi hunters scoured the globe for him Josef Mengele continued to live relatively unimpeded in South America. In 1969 he and the Stammers brought a house on a farm in Caieiras, which is in the São Paulo region of Brazil. In 1971 Wolfgang Gerhard returned to Germany so that his family could receive medical treatment. Knowing that he would no longer need it Gerhard passed his identity card to Mengele. Along with Wolfgang Gerhard, Mengele was later revealed to also have used the pseudonym's Dr Fausto Rindón and Senor Josi Alvers Aspiazu amongst others.

After a falling out, the Stammers left Caieiras in late 1974 and bought a house in São Paulo. Mengele did not accompany them. Despite this break in relations at some point soon after the Stammers bought a bungalow in the Eldorado neighbourhood of São Paulo they rented it out to the ageing Mengele.

Twenty one years after their ski holiday Rolf Mengele visited his father at the bungalow. Here he found an unrepentant Nazi who believed himself to be unfairly pursued as, in his own mind, he had never personally harmed anyone. Mengele trotted out the familiar line that he had only done his duty. Despite only meeting each other on a handful of occasions Rolf and Josef Mengele had corresponded for a period while Josef Mengele lived in South America. Mengele's letters to his son reveal him to be an unrepentant Nazi who considered Hitler to be "the greatest man of the century".

By the time Rolf paid this visit to his father Mengele was a shadow of the man who terrorized his defenseless victims at Auschwitz. Josef Mengele's health had been steadily deteriorating since 1972. Not only did he suffer from high blood pressure but a persistent ear infection affected his balance. Mengele's physical deterioration was hastened by a stroke in 1976. On the 7th of February 1979 while on a visit to friends Wolfram and Liselotte Bossert, who lived in the coastal resort of Bertioga, Mengele suffered another stroke, this time while swimming. It proved to be fatal and he died. Josef Mengele was subsequently buried in Embu das Artes under the name Wolfang

Gerhard. The real Wolfgang Gerhard had died a few months previously in a car accident in Germany.

Mengele's Legacy

Due to the fact that Josef Mengele had lived the latter part of his life under a cloud of secrecy and fake names Simon Wiesenthal continued to believe that he was alive. The search for Mengele continued until 1985. In 1982 a reward of $100,000 was offered for his capture. The search for Josef Mengele received a massive media boost in February 1985 when a mock trial of Mengele was held in Jerusalem. This featured the testimony of over a hundred victims of Mengele's experiments. As Mengele was already dead in the ground this was the closest that his victims and their relatives would get to justice.

While the horrors of the Nazi regime had been known about for many years these testimonies still shocked the world. Shortly after the trial the governments of West Germany, Israel, and the United States launched a coordinated effort to determine Mengele's whereabouts. The Israeli and West German governments, The Washington Times and the Simon Wiesenthal Centre, offered a reward for his capture.

On the 31st of May 1985, local police officers, acting on a tip off received by the West German prosecutor's office, raided the house of Hans Sedlmeier. Sedlmeier had been a lifelong friend of Mengele and had also been employed as the sales manager of Mengele and Sons in Günzburg.

During their exhaustive search the police found a coded address book as well as copies of letters to and from Mengele. One of the letters was from Wolfram and Liselotte Bossert. The contents of the letter notified Hans Sedlmeier of

Josef Mengele's death. The authorities in São Paulo were duly notified and the Bosserts were arrested. Under exhaustive interrogation the couple revealed that Josef Mengele had lived out his last years with them under a false name. They confirmed that after his death he had buried under that same false name. The couple also revealed the location of Mengele's grave.

On the 6th of June 1985 the supposed remains of Josef Mengele were exhumed. An extensive forensic examination confirmed a high degree of probability that this was Mengele's body. Four days later on the 10th of June Rolf Mengele issued a statement confirming that the body was that of his father. Rolf claimed that the news of his father's death had been kept secret in order to protect those who had sheltered him for so many years. In 1992 DNA testing confirmed beyond doubt that the body was that of Josef Mengele. Despite repeated requests the surviving members of the Mengele family have refused to allow for his remains to be repatriated to Germany.

Today the Holocaust is remembered as one of humanity's darkest acts. Josef Mengele, thanks to his actions at Auschwitz Birkenau is perceived as one of the monsters of the Nazi regime. His works and later life have inspired a number of creative works. The novel and subsequent film, The Boys from Brazil (1978) saw Gregory Peck playing a fictional character who was unabashedly based on Josef Mengele. In the story Peck's character establishes a clinic in Brazil. Here he works to produce numerous clones of Adolf Hitler, intent on fulfilling the Nazi's crazed Aryan dream. Meanwhile Josef Mengele's stay in Patagonia was used as the basis of the 2013 Argentinian film The German Doctor with Àlex Brendemühl in the lead role.

Mengele's successful flight to South America has helped to fuel many conspiracy theories that other top Nazi's including Martin Bormann and Adolf Hitler managed to escape the encircled, ruins of Berlin and justice. That other Nazis such as Adolf Eichmann made a similar trip to Mengele has only helped to fuel this belief, as has the fact that Mengele managed to live out the rest of his life without being held account for his actions. These theories have gained traction in recent years.

In February 2010, Alexander Autographs sold a 180-page volume of Mengele's diary at auction for an undisclosed sum to the grandson of a Holocaust survivor. The unidentified previous owner, who had acquired the journals whilst in

Brazil, was reported to be close to the Mengele family. The sale was condemned by a Holocaust survivors' organization as "a cynical act of exploitation aimed at profiting from the writings of one of the most heinous Nazi criminals." Rabbi Marvin Hier of the Simon Wiesenthal Centre was glad to see the diary fall into Jewish hands. "At a time when Ahmadinejad's Iran regularly denies the Holocaust and anti-Semitism and hatred of Jews is back in vogue, this acquisition is especially significant," he said.

In 2011, a further 31 volumes of Mengele's diaries were sold, despite numerous vocal protests, by the same auction house. This time the successful bidder was an undisclosed collector of World War II memorabilia for $245,000.

In 2009, Jorge Camarasa, an Argentine historian, claimed that Josef Mengele had used the Brazilian farming enclave of Candido Godoi as a laboratory to continue his experiments with twins. Camarasa's evidence is mostly based on the fact that from 1963 the number of twins being born in the town and surrounding area skyrocketed. Camarasa claims that numerous people who lived in Candido Godoi told him that Josef, Mengele came to town under the auspices of being a "rural doctor".

These people described how the doctor went from house to house helping with minor medical ailments and withdrawing vials of blood from everyone he treated. How this led to him increasing the birth rate of twins in the area has never been fully explained by those who support the theory. Camarasa's story of Mengele the rural doctor has been disputed by scientists who claim that the isolation of the community has more to do with the increase in the twin's birth rate than the supposed activities of a Nazi doctor on the run. This story illustrates how Josef Mengele and the Nazis still hold a fascination in our imagination and consciousness.

Today Josef Mengele is, like many of his Nazi counterparts, seen as an evil man who committed some of the darkest acts of humanity. The Angel of Death is one of the few high-ranking Nazis who managed to evade justice. Mengele is rightly despised by many, particularly those who either suffered at his hands or who lost family members during the Holocaust. Unlike many men of science who work for the betterment of society and mankind Mengele's depraved works are despised. Instead of revering Mengele and his ilk the world chooses to remember those who lost their lives in the Holocaust, vowing that it should never be allowed to happen again.

As for his remains, the Mengele family has so far refused the repeated requests of the Brazilian authorities to repatriate his remains. They wish to have as little as possible to do with their unrepentant Nazi ancestor. To this day the skeletal remains of Josef Mengele are kept in storage at the São Paulo Institute for Forensic Medicine. Here they are occasionally used as educational aids during forensic medicine courses at the University of São Paulo's medical school. Some may see this as a fitting end for a man who, in his life, was only too happy to use others to further his own scientific understanding.

Printed in Great Britain
by Amazon